PRIDE OF LIONS

Vinod Shankar Nair

PRIDE OF LIONS
Copyright ©Vinod Shankar Nair, 2012

Published in 2012

Published by
Bennett, Coleman & Co. Ltd.,
7, Bahadur Shah Zafar Marg,
New Delhi - 110002

Disclaimer
This book is a complete work of fiction. Every character, name, incident in this book is fictitious. Any similarity or resemblance to the name, character or history of any person living or dead is entirely and purely coincidental and unintentional. The author does not intent to taunt, outrage, insult, wound, or hurt any religion or religious sentiments, beliefs or feelings of any person(s) or class of person(s) or community or caste or creed or gender.

TGB/BCCL will be free from any liability for damages and losses of any nature arising from or related to the content. All disputes are subject to the jurisdiction of competent courts in Delhi.

Edited, Designed, Marketed & Distributed by

Times Group Books Times Group Books
(A division of Bennett, Coleman & Co. Ltd.)
Times Annexe, 9-10, Bahadur Shah Zafar Marg, New Delhi-110002

Printed at: Nutech Photolithographers

ISBN 978-93-80942-66-7

Price: ₹249

This book is dedicated to:

MY BELOVED MOTHER

FOREWORD

We live in a highly charged and transient society today where everything is fleeting and nothing can be taken for granted. Given this reality, it is my sincere belief that the greatest asset an individual can have is a strong set of values.

One who is armed with a strong value system can lead a life free of guilt, remorse and regret. Such a person can also withstand emotional, mental, physical, cultural, financial or social turbulence.

It took a measure of courage for me to write this book and it will take you an equal measure of courage to read it. All I ask of you my dear reader is that you keep an open mind till the very last word of the book.

ACKNOWLEDGEMENTS

A. Sankara Pillai & N. Bhargavi Amma: My role models

Mom & Dad: I love you

Miss Tulip Joshi:
This book may never have been completed without your consistent encouragement, support and light.

Mr. Veer Vinod Nair: My pride, my faith and my legacy

Mr. Brijesh Singh: Thank you for your honesty, time and support. You are a personification of the word 'friend'.

Mr. Gaggandip Singh Brar

The Indian Army: My education

1

A nagging restlessness gnawed at young Kimmaya from within but she couldn't identify what was causing it. All she knew was that it began the moment she had stepped into class this morning. Even the usually interesting class teacher seemed to drone on tonelessly, her words only aggravated the unease.

Kimmaya looked out the window of her classroom at the bright day outside where she could see a line of trees beyond the vast football field. It was the beginning of May and sweltering heat had set in. She thanked God she was born after air conditioners had been invented. The football field used to be completely green but now it was half brown, summer also made the trees bloom orange flowers known as *Gulmohar* or 'Flame of the Forest'. The sky was a clear light blue with no clouds in sight, the sun shone high above reflecting off car and rooftops. From where she sat, the cars, buildings, movie hoardings, grounds and greenery formed a riot of vibrant colours like a bouquet of assorted flowers. She was willing to leave the cool comfort of her seat and face the soaring temperature outdoors to circumvent her inexplicable stifling feeling.

She decided to run a checklist to identify the source of this inner discomfort. Her wavy shoulder-length hair had been left open and was perfectly in place – nothing wrong there; she discretely pulled out a pocket mirror and sneaked a glance at the sharp featured lean face looking back at her with sparkling eyes from the mirror. No makeup; didn't need any – nothing wrong there either. She looked down at her clothes, she wore a 'V'-neck, white, long-sleeve tee shirt that clung to her athletic frame, matched with khaki cargo pants and her favourite all-terrain boots. All okay! Body odour? Bloating? Nope. All good there as well.

Convinced that her discomfort didn't stem from her appearance, she looked around and about her at her environment. The seat she sat in was her usual one and as usual she was flanked by her two best friends Brij on her left and Sandy on her right (Brij, short for Brijesh Singh and Sandy, short for Sadiq Shah).

Could Brij or Sandy be the cause of her restlessness?

Kim, Brij and Sandy were childhood friends who had grown up together, gone to the same school and lived close to each other. They were in and out of each other's homes all the time. Their equation included cutthroat rivalry; competing at every level in sports, athletics, academics and everything else. They were the brightest students in this class; well-mannered, unapologetically intelligent and very well spoken. All three came from well-heeled and reputed families.

Sandy was an only child from a family of jewellers which catered to the cream of society; his father, a Gujarati who ran their business was highly educated and well travelled, he liked to keep a low profile and was respected for his subtlety. Sandy's mother was of Muslim lineage, she was like royalty, known as one of the finest hosts in the social circuit. They had met on campus when they were both students at Oxford; it was love at first sight for them that resulted in marital bliss.

Sandy was fair, tall and heavy; he loved debating, movies and food. His love for Indian delicacies like butter chicken and biryani showed on his waistline but he didn't care, it was worth it.

Like Sandy, Kim too was an only child. Kim's father was an iconic public figure; a war veteran decorated for gallantry, he had founded a business of strategy consulting and had developed it into a global giant. His clientele included companies, film stars, politicians and other luminaries. He was a revered master strategist, the man with the Midas touch. He was a celebrity of sorts with the media following his every move, covering all his appearances and activities. Kim and her father doted on each other.

Kim was a natural athlete who loved running and long jumps, records broken by her in her school remained untouched till date. Taught by her father, she was an expert mountain climber and trekker, she knew how to start a fire, hunt, skin and cook in the wilderness. At her young age, she had already done skydiving, bungee jumping and mountain climbing. She loved kickboxing, reading, writing, debates and chess. Kim was a livewire who radiated intelligence, beauty and energy all at the same time.

Unlike Kim and Sandy, Brij was the eldest of three siblings, his mother was an accomplished neuro-surgeon whose services were highly sort after and his father was the legal head of a Fortune 500 multinational conglomerate. They were a highly respected and close-knit family who were role models of success and happiness.

Taking the best of both his parents, Brij had a way with statistical data; he was a human encyclopedia of information. When in need of facts or data, students often turned to him. His strengths didn't end there; he was also a gifted sportsperson passionate about football. A complete outdoors person, Brij dreamt of being a soldier or a sports star and was unceasingly game for any activity. His general knowledge was phenomenal but he liked to keep away from the eclectic debates that Sandy and Kim often entered into. He was happy providing information on topics but rarely argued because he believed that facts made statements beyond contention.

Thanks to Kim, Sandy and Brij's friendship, their parents too had grown close to each other, they were now like one large family.

All three were erudite, sharp as knives, thick as thieves and never missed a beat. Together they were formidable; Sandy's eye for detail was accorded to the jeweller's blood that ran in his veins. Kim's ability to grasp new concepts and learn in leaps and bounds based on instinct and gut feel was inherited from her father. Brij's ability to pop up accurate and relevant data out of thin air made them an excellent team.

They had their share of arguments too, for two days now Kim and Sandy had been arguing over a project assigned to them, which had to be presented on Monday but it had come to a point where they both agreed to disagree. Their dissention on this project was unlikely to end in the near future. These arguments did bother Kim, their friendship was beyond being shaken or stirred by such issues. So she decided that her discomfort hadn't been caused by her two best friends either.

Kim now looked in front at the oversized class teacher who sat in her chair, girth spilling out from all sides. Mrs. Margaret Parker, fondly known as 'Maggie', was an educationist with over thirty years of teaching experience tucked safely under her belt. Kim noted that Maggie seemed to be in a bit of a hurry to wrap up and leave the class. The remaining sessions were scheduled to be taken by Ms. Vaz but rumour had it that she was ill and hadn't turned up at all. possibility was that there would be no more class and they'd pack up for the weekend. 'Good!' Kim thought, at least she'd get to go home early; she had no intention of staying on with this persistent unease.

Kim then saw the big banner hanging six feet in the air, stretched across the class wall behind Maggie. It had 'HAPPY MOTHER'S DAY' written on it in capital letters with gold dust with coloured hearts sprinkled across it. She instantly knew why she had been uneasy all day.

Kim's mother had passed away a few hours after delivering her due to complications in childbirth. She had grown up with her Dad; they were best friends and reversed roles often. She monitored his lifestyle and ensured that he wouldn't overwork.

He on the other hand played mother and father to her round the clock. Their relationship was of mutual love and dependence. Her days were packed with sports, studies, friends and time for Dad; her life was blissful and she had nothing to complain about but once a year on Mother's Day, she couldn't help but want to hurry home and be with her Dad because no one meant more to her in the world than him... especially on Mother's Day.

Her reverie was interrupted when Brij slid a piece of paper across the desk to her. She looked at him questioningly, took and read it 'let's play some tennis and watch a movie tonight? Check with Sandy too'. Kim slid it to her right where Sandy sat; he looked at it and scribbled on it before sliding it back. Kim looked at what he had written, he cancelled 'tennis' with several forceful strokes and replaced it with 'butter chicken and rumali roti dinner'... typical of Sandy! Kim passed on the note back to Brij who scribbled on it again and passed it back to Kim. It now read 'Let's do whatever Kim wants.' Sandy reached across and wrote a big 'Yes' on it. Kim wrote on it this time, 'Sorry already promised dinner with Dad tonight but why are you guys being so nice to me today?' Sandy quickly grabbed the paper and wrote again on it 'Because it's Mother's day and you are our Mom!'

Brij and Kim read Sandy's reply together and both laughed out loudly before realizing that the class teacher Maggie was staring, willing them to stop what they were doing.

Maggie asked "Would the three of you like to share the reason for your mirth?"

"No, Ma'am!" the three musketeers said in unison and put their heads down pretending to work.

Maggie had watched Kim, Brij and Sandy pass the scrap of paper around but she had chosen to ignore because they were her favourite students. She was forced to intervene after they laughed loudly and interrupted the entire class. She leaned forward and looked over the rim of her spectacles at the eighteen students sitting in front of her, they were a mixed batch of local and international students in their teens; razor sharp young minds bursting with energy, ideas and waiting to explode on to the world.

The energy exuded by these youngsters was palpable. Maggie's Reiki healer would have loved to sit at the back of the class to simply soak in their strength and feel young. Then again, Maggie had told her Reiki healer that kids this age carry a lot of baggage. They are neither children nor adults; they understand logic and question everything. Their intelligence enables them to instantly differentiate between right and wrong, good and bad as black and white but their lack of exposure and maturity limits their ability to fully comprehend shades of grey and concepts like trust and perception. They have yet to understand that one size does not fit all and hence, powers of discretion need to be used while applying rules to different people. Maggie often said that life maybe tough when you are a teen but it's even tougher when you have to deal with so many teens every day of your life.

On her maternal side, Maggie's family was unique in that

for the past five generations they had consistently delivered only baby girls. There had not yet been a male child born in the family. This tradition was upheld again a week ago when Maggie's daughter delivered a beautiful bony baby girl. To add to the joy, today was 'Mothers Day', and that was for obvious reasons a big day in Maggie's family. All the ladies would get together and celebrate motherhood with a wonderful wine and cheese evening followed by a sumptuous dinner. This time the celebration was at Maggie's home. She had to hurry up and get there to make sure all the preparations were in order. With her daughter's recent delivery, this Mother's Day would indeed be a big celebration!

She glanced at the wall clock above the students; the bell would sound soon. She looked back at them and spoke. "You are scheduled for sessions with Miss Vaz for the rest of the day. However, she hasn't come in today. So, I should simply let you go home early…"

There was an instant rumble in the classroom as the students perked up. She could see them nudge and whisper to at each other. They simply couldn't wait to get out.

"Sssssshhh! Hush!!!!"She raised her voice and the room instantly fell silent. She looked at them carefully before continuing.

"However, since the weekend starts now and you all have to present your projects on Monday, I suggest you use this free time to do some preparation before you leave. I have asked the principal's office to send across a volunteer to provide you with any support you may need. Someone should be here shortly."

She watched their backs slump as they resigned themselves to their fate of having to stay in the room.

"As assigned, you will work in teams of three and you will present your projects together as a team on Monday. Does everyone know who their partners are?"

Students looked across at their partners and nodded back.

She continued, "Any questions or clarifications anyone?"

Three hands came up to get her attention. Maggie picked the first one, a young girl who would no doubt soon bloom into a timeless beauty. "Yes Ishra?" She asked.

Ishra stood up and spoke. "Ma'am my project is 'Clean Future means Green Future' and my partners are Saumit and Nadia. I have a request."

"What's your request?" Maggie asked.

"Ma'am I can't work with Saumit."

Maggie looked at Nadia and Saumit. Nadia giggled uncontrollably and Saumit sat with a sheepish grin in his seat; it was obvious that they knew about Ishra's dissatisfaction. She then looked back at Ishra, "Why, what's the problem in working with Saumit?"

Ishra's response was quick, "He's very irritating, I can't stand him. He keeps on eating with loud crunching noises and then farts like a blow horn."

Maggie managed to keep a straight face. Though most of them had become half adults, they were still half children. She turned to Saumit and spoke sternly. "Saumit you will learn to be more considerate towards others. You will also be more sensitive and hygienic. Any more complaints about your hygiene or etiquette and it will be a month of detention for you. Is that understood?"

"Yes ma'am," an embarrassed Saumit responded.

Maggie then looked back at Ishra and spoke. "Engaging differing opinions and personalities and yet arriving at productive outcomes is necessary in the real world that awaits you Ishra. We must all communicate, co-exist and work in harmony with others who differ from us in many ways. That's an integral part of your learning on this exercise. Hence your request is denied."

The remaining two hands still up were of Kim and Sandy. Maggie felt a nervous twitch in her left eye. It was fun watching the three musketeers compete with and take digs at each other but when they united and started exploring a subject, she broke into a sweat. There was hardly anything that Brij didn't have data about. For the rest, Sandy's hawk eye grasped almost everything and if in the unlikely event something did slip by Brij and Sandy, it was instantly picked by Kim's gut feel and instinct. Together, they were a nightmare for Maggie.

An interesting system was used to decide partners for these projects. Names of colours were printed on little neatly folded sheets of paper that were placed in a jar. Each student picked a sheet, after that, they read aloud the colour printed inside. Those who had the same colour mentioned on their sheets formed a team. Brij smacked his forehead when he found that like him, Sandy and Kim had picked yellow. The rest of the class guffawed loudly; no one could wait to see what would happen next.

"Yes?" Maggie asked, dreading what was going to come.

Sandy spoke first. "Ma'am can we please have a different topic for our project?"

Then Maggie turned her gaze to Kim who spoke up without hesitation. "Or a different partner, even Saumit will do. He may lack etiquette but at least his loyalties are clear"

"Why?" Maggie asked. What's your subject?"

It was again Sandy who spoke first. "The project assigned to us is: 'My Country, My Pride'."

"Okay and?" Maggie egged him on.

Sandy said, "Ma'am we spent the last few days researching this topic."

Since Sandy normally spoke sense, Maggie paid attention to him. He continued, "Ma'am we've found a lot of content on our country's past that's to be proud of. Many inventions, many firsts, a rich old culture, an advanced society and lots more that really makes us proud Ma'am."

"So what's the problem Sandy?" Maggie asked.

Sandy continued "Ma'am our past is awesome but it's the present and future that's got me stumped."

"What do you mean?" Maggie persisted.

"Well Ma'am there are a few things that bother me: We have a crumbling infrastructure; leave alone supporting us, it is battling to simply exist! We have community, caste and religious divides everywhere. Most of India has restrictive, inhibiting lifestyles but strangely ours is the fastest growing population in the world - don't you think there's something's missing there?

We are probably the most corrupt nation as of now; politicians, mafia-builder nexus, skyrocketing inflation. As if that isn't enough, we still have archaic laws being implemented by a lethargic justice system that begins hearing cases twenty years after they've been filed and then go on for another twenty years before they conclude.

Our system is one that protects captured terrorists better than it does its own taxpaying public. I am of course referring to the way an Ajmal Kasab is guarded and fed while an Anna Hazare is thrown in prison. Speaking of terrorists, we are the favourite target for terrorists from across the world. No protection or cover.

What about terror and extradition? What's our policy there? Our heads of state personally escorted captured terrorists to other countries! The US and Israel hunt down and eliminate even potential threats to their way of life no matter where in the world they maybe and we? Individuals known to have funded and masterminded blasts here openly live like kings a few kilometers beyond our borders and we do nothing!

That isn't all, we have a nonexistent or chronically weak foreign policy. Whenever anything earth-shattering happens anywhere in the world like a war or a coup, India's standard reaction is that 'We are very concerned and monitoring the situation carefully.' We hardly ever take a stand.

How could I forget our internal problems that we are helpless against? Burgeoning population, dirt, no hygiene, no sanitation, no unemployment benefits, make what you can when you can but once you stop earning, there's no one to protect or care for the old and poor. I don't even need to mention the omnipresent brain drain. Any and everyone who's educated and well off simply migrates to Europe, US or Canada and for good reason too! There are things people in most parts of the world can take for granted but not us, not here, here one needs acrobatic skills to simply cross the road...any road! Getting to the other side is a traumatic ordeal, every time I reach safely I say a silent prayer of gratitude... I could go on Ma'am."

Maggie was speechless. She stared back, her mind digesting everything that Sandy had said...processing the information to come up with a good answer. The tough part was that everything Sandy had said was true and she agreed with him fully but she had picked this topic herself, she had made students prepare projects for years. The classroom, she and the topic remained the same, times had changed, thirty years had whizzed by without her realizing the changes that had crept in discretely everywhere. Students had become much smarter and more outspoken, with Sandy's assault, the topic suddenly seemed obsolete, out of place and almost childish.

Maggie quickly considered her options; maybe she could back down and give them a new topic? No! Not at this point; it would make her appear foolish and set a bad precedent that would undermine her standing in the class, students would argue about everything and there would be no end to it! A confrontation with Sandy and Kim backed by Brij's data would definitely end in her being trampled upon in front of all her students. She could feel her palms begin to sweat, she knew she had been cornered and needed to buy time, her throat felt parched. She had to find a way out without admitting defeat.

She maintained her external composure; didn't bat an eyelid, instead she looked around for respite but it was still Sandy who spoke again "Brij agrees with me, all the stats I have are his," he said. To which Brij nodded somberly, his eyes fixed on Maggie. Sandy ploughed on, "Kim disagrees with me; she says our present is a transient reality and our future is bright."

Maggie felt a wave of relief as a load lifted off her shoulders; Kim's disagreement was like a ray of hope for her, if Kim had agreed with Sandy and if Brij had joined them, Maggie knew she'd be outclassed. She cleared her choked throat and blurted, "Go on…"

"The problem Ma'am, is that Kim has very little data to back her case. We can't present a project based on gut feel or hope. We need facts to support every statement. For every single point in her favour, I've dug up ten other weaknesses to bury her."

Just then the class bell rang. Maggie almost jumped with joy but her experience had taught her to be stoical. 'Saved by the bell' she thought. She quickly gathered her things and stood up before she replied.

"Identity and pride are very serious issues facing the nation today and that's why I've chosen this topic as a challenge to test your IQ and resourcefulness. You may discuss this in more detail and take tips from the volunteer who will come now to keep you busy through the rest of today. I am off, have a nice weekend and see you all with your project presentations on Monday. Bye now." So saying Maggie dashed for the door and her freedom with a speed that surprised everyone.

Sandy looked clearly dissatisfied with Maggie's response. As soon she left, chaos exploded in the room. All at once, there was chatter, laughter, things being thrown and names being called. Ten minutes later there was still no sign of the volunteer teacher; students were getting increasingly restless. Some were up and about, mischief levels were rising when a few excited students whispered audibly, "Someone's coming, someone's coming. Get back to your places." There was an instant hustle as everyone rushed back to their seats.

2

A moment later, the door opened and a woman in her late fifties or early sixties entered the room, from thereon it was as if time stood still. There was something magical about her; her platinum hair was thick, full and long. She was about five feet seven inches tall and dressed in a simple white sari with an orange border and a green blouse; she was a picture of aristocratic elegance.

Her face was captivating, there wasn't a single crease on her smooth flawless, dusky complexion, no wrinkles but a few laugh lines for sure; her eyes were bright, twinkling blue and her smile was infectious. No one could take their eyes off as they followed her every move as she reached centre stage.

The class waited breathlessly for her. When she was settled, she stood in front of them and looked at every single student for a moment before she finally spoke. Her penetrating, hypnotic blue eyes were like a missile locking system on a moving target, once contact was established each and every student was frozen and unable to break free; her magnetism was irresistible.

Her voice was warm and comforting yet it had an inescapable strength to it. "Namaste!" she said. "Good evening girls and boys, my name is Indu and we are going to spend the next few hours together. Apologies for being late. I was caught up in a discussion about your impending projects on my way here. It has been suggested that we use this opportunity to help with your projects for Monday. The internet is available and you can also feel free to ask or discuss anything you want with me."

The class rustled into activity as students began to switch on their laptops, notebooks and e-pads. Chatter amongst them also started up and the class hummed into activity.

Kim and Sandy looked at each other. They had a distinct 'Should we or shouldn't we?' expression sketched on their faces. They looked at Indu and realized she was already looking at them as if she knew that they wanted to ask her something. She nodded at them and smiled enigmatically, encouraging them to speak.

Sandy started, "Ma'am I had asked this question to Mrs. Parker already, our topic is 'My Country, My Pride'. I've been able to find a lot to be proud of about our country's past but almost nothing in our present or likely future."

Indu listened completely, her congenial smile firmly in place. She then looked at the entire class and addressed everyone. "Sandy has an excellent question backed by some valid points about corruption, population, hygiene, safety and a few more. Would anyone like to answer Sandy's question?"

Sandy was surprised that she knew his name and knew all his points, he guessed that Mrs. Parker would have briefed Indu in detail but Kim didn't waste any time pondering, she spoke up instantly. "One of the fastest growing economies in the world," she said. Another quipped, "Probably the only country not to be hit by recession in the last ten years."

Sandy responded with "What's the use of such a growth rate when inflation is much higher and farmers are still starving to death or committing suicides?"

Yet another spoke up. "We are not an aggressive country, we are a gentle giant with nuclear power but we don't attack anyone, we are peace loving and known for our tolerance."

Sandy had a relaxed expression; he had been through all this before. He responded quickly, "Don't attack? Or can't attack? There's a difference between the two. The best we do is express 'shock and anguish' and promise to retaliate but after countless attacks on the very beacons of our nation, we still sit twiddling our thumbs and do nothing. When it comes to going nuclear, why even talk when we don't have the spine to stand up even in non-nuclear situations? Besides, the world will gang up against us if we use nuclear weapons."

Kim ignored Sandy and spoke again. "Also, probably the most intelligent people on earth, inventors of the Zero digit, Yoga, Ayurved and Chess."

Sandy shot back instantly. "That's again in the past. I am

not questioning past achievements, let's stick to our shaky present and dubious future. Our topic is 'My Country; my Pride' not 'My Past; my Pride'."

Ishra spoke excitedly. "Largest democracy, person of Italian origin heading the country's oldest political party. A minority community person as Prime Minister. We have had ladies as President and Prime Minister. Several of our Presidents have been from minority communities like Zakir Hussain, Fakhruddin Ali Ahmed, Gyani Zail Singh and Abul Kalam. Some of our leading film stars are from minority communities, what greater statement of mass acceptance? And all this long, long before America elected a coloured President. We exemplify the word democracy."

Sandy spoke up. "True! Yet none of that can take away the communal riots, honour killings, rampant corruption, racism or female foeticide! Isn't there anyway to check this?"

Soon the debate petered out and the class fell silent with only Sandy still standing tall, holding his ground.

3

Sandy said, "This situation makes me angry, I'm sure there are others who share my rage and believe me that's the only solution. If this anger increases and spreads among people, we will have an Egypt-like situation on our hands. Or even like the Russian or French revolutions. Maybe that will resolve these issues. Anger could help, what do you think Ma'am?"

Indu was silent for a moment before she spoke. "I suppose you are right when you say ire may spread and cause a revolution but I don't think that it is a solution to anything."

"Why not Ma'am?" Sandy asked. "It is a great motivator and some people respond only to extremes. Well-channelled anger can deliver superb solutions."

"Well Sandy everything you say is true, anger may motivate us to take a stand against negatives and injustices but it may not be the best way to deal with them. We must stand for virtues and principles rather than against wrong doings. The difference is a fine line and crossing this line is enough to make a person lose focus in life, make a country go down the drain and destroy many, many lives."

"What's wrong with standing against something that's incorrect?" Ishra asked. Isn't it okay to get angry and take a stand against poverty and corruption?"

"Yes Ishra but I suggest that we should stop being reactive and start being proactive. If you know what you stand for then you will automatically remove obstacles. Revolutions often start because they stand against injustice, tyranny, oppression but once they finish overthrowing the regime, they aren't sure what they stand for. Take a long term, non-reactive view and decide what you believe in, it helps to keep things in perspective and not lose focus or get carried away with the tide. It helps if you know what you are standing for along with what you are standing against.

So instead of standing against poverty, corruption and terror, we will be better off standing for abundance, equal opportunity, transparency and accountability."

The class was silent as the young minds made sense of the weighty words that had been delivered on them. Finally Sandy spoke again. "Can't argue with what you said Ma'am but it still doesn't address my issue of pride in the nation."

Indu smiled and responded, "Pride, love, honour, dignity, respect and loyalty have nothing to do with statistics. These are human values that exist in a higher realm way beyond basal intelligence levels of logic and data."

Young minds churned hard to fathom Indu's statement. She then continued, "What sets humans apart from other species is that we have evolved beyond basal instincts, simple logic-based calculations and developed other faculties like humour, foresight, honour, etc. And the differences between us and our machines like computers is that we have self-respect, loyalty, love, compassion and pride. Take these away and what difference do we have? So addressing the issue of pride with statistics and data is like asking an illiterate person to read and interpret a book."

Sandy was forced to concede temporarily so he nodded in agreement. Brij however, didn't like what he heard; his reputation and personality was constructed on his ability to reproduce factual information. He stayed silent.

"What do you suggest for pride in our country Ma'am?" Kim asked, "I feel sad that many people are unaware of concepts like pride and patriotism."

"I wish it were simple Kim…" Indu responded, surprising Kim that Indu knew her name too "…pride and respect have nothing to do with verifiable data and facts. We must be aware of, acknowledge and tackle real issues facing us systematically and scientifically but we must also be proud of who we are and where we come from. Please don't interlink the two. I agree with every single issue that Sandy has raised and I also understand that solving such complex issues takes multi-pronged and patient remedies."

"What do you mean? Please explain," Brij said.

"Well Brij, we cannot eradicate poverty unless our

neighbouring countries are also better off, otherwise the influx of refugees will never stop. As long as poverty and lifestyle disparities exist, so will the scope for exploitation of youngsters to take to violence."

"We will have to act patiently at several levels to address these issues. Our solutions lie in participative wealth, responsibility towards each other as cohabitants of the same home and that home is earth. I'm talking about participative wealth and cohabitation across species not only nation, religion or community. One of the main solutions along with a few others is education and by education I don't mean literacy. I am talking about core values such as humanity, loyalty, respect, communication, integrity and a few other such indispensables that we are seeing less and less of today."

Ishra interrupted, "Values as in? Please explain."

Indu continued, "Coming back to Sandy and Kim's topic on pride, values are not connected to logic, values are anything that you hold dear to you. They form the skeleton around which your character is built; they are the beacons that guide you through the thunderstorms of life." There was a moment of silence after she paused as the class grappled with what had been said.

This time it was Anita who spoke. "Sorry Ma'am I didn't understand. Please explain again."

Indu listened, her bright smile sprang back in place and she spoke. "Life doesn't come with a handbook or an operating manual, it's full of surprises. Rules change, situations change, people change and we ourselves change all the time. We are each tossed into situations that we have to make the best of with the resources we have. It's like having to play a game with the cards dealt to us. We have to jostle, negotiate with what we have and still come out on top.

However, there are some things in our lives that we must never compromise on, they are non-negotiable. If we do let go of these, it will be like selling our soul to the devil. Values add colour and to us as individuals, they are unique to each of us and give us direction from within. For example, for someone their greatest value maybe honesty, for another it maybe respect, yet for a third person it may be the truth or their parent's happiness. There's no saying which is better or worse, values are very personal and cannot be generalized.

Our values are like lighthouses in a stormy sea, telling us where to steer. They give us clarity on what's important and what is negotiable. Values are the fabric of our personality based on which our life is lived. Any person with clarity about their values faces minimum internal conflict and can ride through seemingly difficult decisions with ease."

"You mean values are our principles?" Ishra asked.

"Values are at the core of our principles." Indu responded.

This time most of the young faces before her lit up with understanding. Several nodded in agreement.

Indu continued, "Like I said before, values aren't based on logic, they reside at the core of your being; your conscience pulls you towards them. Values should be questioned before adoption not after."

"Logic is essential to us and our decision-making process, it is an integral rung of our intelligence but it isn't the final step. Human beings are blessed with gifts such as humour, honour and artistic creativity that reside in a zone beyond logic, arithmetic and computing. Using these gifts takes us forward in leaps and bounds. Arithmetic is a great base to start constructing your thoughts and assumptions from but beyond that, I'd say it's meant for mobile phones, computers and calculators. Let's take another example. Let's say love for our mother, it defies logic and can push a person to any extreme. Got it?"

An awkward silence hung in the room till Delnaz Pestonji cut in, "Ma'am you need to give another example because Kim doesn't have a mother."

Indu looked back at Kim who nodded slightly. Indu said, "Kim's mother hasn't died. She has simply passed on to a different form. She still lives within her family and friends and her soul will exist forever." Indu's already radiant personality now seemed to glow some more.

Hearing this Kim felt like a ton of bricks had been removed from her head and she had been set free. Her restlessness and discomfort vanished! She felt light and alive!

Sandy stole a quick glance at Kim. He could have sworn he saw her quickly wipe a tear and felt his own eyes well up.

Indu continued, "Your mother may not be the fittest, prettiest, richest or the best cook you know but despite all her flaws and shortcomings you still love her the most. You don't need statistics to convince you to love your parents, siblings or even your friends. That's rising beyond computing. Loyalty, honour and friendship too are beyond logic and so is love and patriotism.

Your country is also your mother, she has given you birth, nurtured and provided all you have. You don't need certifications or laurels to love her and feel for her; you just do. Achievements should add to your joy but lack of achievements should not take away self-respect. I am not condoning corruption, communalism or any of our other shortcomings. We should identify our areas of improvement and get to work on them but it still has nothing to do with pride, dignity and self respect.

You don't choose to love your parents based on their bank balances, you simply do! Self-confidence and faith are along the same lines. You don't need to ride in a fancy car to increase your faith or confidence. If you have faith, you have faith. If you are a confident person, then you simply are regardless of what you wear or what you possess. Confidence that comes from wearing a branded watch or carrying a fancy handbag or wearing a label is not confidence, that's false security and peer or social pressure that must be done away with."

"Wow!!" a student named Ashiana Mehta said loudly and clapped in applause. The whole class joined her clapping. Ishra said, "Ma'am you have the prettiest eyes I have ever seen."

"This is amazing! Why didn't any of us think of this?" Sandy asked.

"Because times have changed...," Indu said, "...earlier one had to first achieve something meaningful before being celebrated and famous. Nowadays, you have to be famous and celebrated regardless of your achievements. This is a worldwide media phenomenon not limited to any country. Today popular reality TV shows take convicted felons, known drug abusers and scandalously infamous people as participants to get viewership. So the message sent to the new generation is 'Get famous, it doesn't matter how.' That's where values get diluted and we lose our pride, respect and humanity."

Every student sat mesmerized as Indu spoke, her deep blue eyes searing through them, reaching and soothing their very soul as she continued, "Does this mean we have stopped producing quality people as a nation? Does that mean we have stopped producing heroes altogether?

No. There are role models and heroes all around us and in us. We encounter them every single day in our normal lives. It's these heroes that define India and what she stands for. In fact right in this room, we have achievers, visionaries, heroes – present here and now."

Students felt the hair on the back of their necks stand and goose bumps all over. They had never felt so charged or passionate about their nation before.

Brij asked, "If each individual's values can be different, how do we go about identifying our own? And how do we educate people on values?"

Indu responded, "Brilliant question Brij, probably the toughest one to answer; every individual's values are personal and to be made by themselves from their own inner calling, experience, knowledge, upbringing, socio-economic situation, instincts, priorities, etc. However, since we are all from a similar bandwidth here in this room, we may find a lot of similarities in our values. I would rather not suggest values to you as you are intelligent enough to construct your own. Someone once said, don't feed a hungry man fish, instead you teach him to catch fish and he'll learn to take care of himself for ever. So I'd rather not suggest or give you any values but I'll guide you on how to identify and live by your own values."

"How?" Brij asked.

"I can share a story with you, once I've done that, you comb through the entire tale and it will help you arrive at some of your values. What do you think?"

"Sounds like a plan!" Brij responded with gusto and several other students agreed.

Indu said, "Okay let's go ahead then, listen to the entire

story carefully, don't miss a beat and then think hard about it from all possible angles. May I start?"

"Yes Ma'am!" was the excited chorus in the classroom.

"Okay, wonderful!" Indu sparkled.

"What's it about? I mean what genre is it?" Ayesha asked.

Indu replied, "It's a love story Ayesha." She paused, looked at all the young eager faces in front of her and continued, "I hope the love, thoughts, words and actions of the people in this story will touch your heart the way they've touched mine.

The incident I am going to tell you about took place over a span of five days in August 1991 in the Line of Control of the Indian Border."

Ayesha interrupted again. "Ma'am two more questions, first, how do you know all our names?"

"Ayesha my child, of course I know the names of all my children! What's your second question?"

Ayesha flashed a delighted smile and said, "Wow! Never met a teacher who knew all our names without several introductions! Thank you Ma'am, you make us feel special! And my second question is that I am a huge fan of love stories…does it have a name? I mean, does your story have a name?"

"Yes it does Ayesha, it's called 'Pride of Lions'".

"That's a fascinating name! Why is it called that?" Ayesha asked again.

Sandy interrupted loudly, "Shut up Ayesha. We all want to hear the story not you so please stop it…enough with the questions!"

Indu laughed, "Ayesha, I will look to you for an answer after we are done with the story. So shall we start?"

The entire class responded with an enthusiastic and resounding "YES!!"

Indu began. "Let me give you a background first."

4

The marketing campaign for Indian tourism worldwide refers to India as 'Incredible India'. Whoever coined this term was quite accurate. India is a visually dazzling, mentally stimulating, emotionally rich and spiritually transcendental place. It is the paradox of paradoxes where the most outrageous fashion trends from Milan and Paris harmoniously coexist with the most conservative styles from other ends of the world. While couples break away from tradition and live-in together in cities like Bangalore, Pune and Mumbai, others are torched or beaten to death by their own family members for as little as establishing 'eye contact' with the opposite sex.

The geographical variations are just as spectacular. India shares borders with several countries and spans picturesque topography stretching from Kashmir in the North to Assam, Meghalaya, Manipur, Tripura and Nagaland in the East continuing through other beautiful states like Uttar Pradesh, Uttaranchal, Bihar, Gujarat and Rajasthan, then, onwards to Maharashtra, Karnataka, Andhra Pradesh, Tamil Nadu and Kerala in the South.

Northern India is a visual treat; it is blessed with the river Ganges and the Himalayas. The stark beauty is breathtaking to say the least, the highest peak in the world, Mount Everest, is part of the Himalayan mountain ranges.

The middle regions of the Himalayas are known as the Pir Panjal ranges. They stretch through Himachal Pradesh, Jammu, Kashmir and go beyond India's borders as well.

Kashmir is so beautiful that the Mughal emperor Jehangir wrote and I quote *Gar firdaus, ruhe zamin ast, hamin asto, hamin asto, hamin ast*. Loosely translated, that means: 'If there is a paradise on the face of the earth, it is here, it is here, it is here.'

The extreme beauty of these mountains is matched only by their unforgiving nature. They ruthlessly take lives without warning and remorse. Avalanches, lightning strikes, thunderstorms, landslides and flash floods are some of the dangers that this terrain presents. The weather is unpredictable and merciless. These ranges are also the breeding ground for terrible human violence. For centuries, marauders traversed the Pir Panjal ranges to enter mainland India and loot settlers there. In recent years, these mountain ranges are a battleground where Indian armed forces prevent terrorists from entering the country. The harsh climate, freezing cold weather, poor visibility and undulating ground make it an ideal place to sneak in arms, ammunition and death.

Our story, set in this beautiful backdrop took place over a span of five days in August 1991. So travel through time with me as we spin the clock back by two decades."

Indu continued, "To the North West of Jammu, about a

day's drive along a very treacherous mountainous road, lay a small border town named Doonch. It was connected to the rest of India by a strategically vital bridge named Kalai Bridge – *kalai* in Hindi means wrist. It was a sleepy town with a few residents and a noisy marketplace populated by hardy, helpful and very friendly locals. Their buoyant nature revealed no trace of the hardships they faced. Cut off from the rest of India, placed along the volatile border, the people of this town lived with death as their constant companion. Losing life and limb to landmines, heavy artillery shelling, bomb blasts and regular terror strikes were part of their daily lives. Militarily, Doonch was the headquarters of a vital brigade of the Indian Army at that time commanded by Brigadier Sher Ali Khan, a thorough gentleman known for his outstanding intelligence and love for the local people.

A couple of hours drive from Doonch towards the Indian border was where the tarred road ended, from there on it was a dangerous dirt track upwards into some of the most beautiful mountains on earth. An hour and a half of such bumpy driving later was Tindi. It was a tiny dwelling place where a few shepherds tended to their flock. The only vehicular movement there was that of Indian army trucks and jeeps grinding their way up the challenging mountain tracks.

At no point in all this could you possibly escape the beauty of the mountainside as the snowcapped peaks reflected the sun and covered expanses of green and brown mountain faces. The mountain air crackled with purity, there was absolutely no pollution.

Two hours walk downwards from Tindi through the rugged mountains was the Line of Control referred to as LOC. It is a volatile and constantly changing boundary shared with our neighbouring country. Unlike the International Border, the LOC is not sacrosanct; there are no pillars or markings.

Troops of both countries take their defenses as aggressively forward as possible. In this aggression they sometimes even capture and occupy each other's outposts.

Unclaimed land between the two countries is called 'No man's Land.' Anyone or anything seen moving in No man's Land is instantly shot at and killed by either side.

There was never a dull moment. Apart from each other, both sides had to deal with a common adversary and that was the lethal and unpredictable weather which often took more casualties than either side.

22ND AUGUST 1991

Ring Contour was a strategically vital post held by an Indian infantry unit of the Kumaon regiment. Ring Contour was so important because of its shape and positioning; it was a monolithic hill feature situated on the Line of Control. Who ever held it, commanded a direct view into the other's territory.

During the last two years, the enemy had tried to occupy it several times but had failed every time with heavy casualties. In early July 1991, the soldiers of Kumaon began to pull out and were being relieved by another infantry of the

Punjab Regiment. Handing and taking over was a long and tedious process anywhere but this especially so for an infantry unit of over seven hundred men spread over kilometers of undulating mountains.

The handover had just happened and the Punjabi soldiers were still getting a feel of their new responsibilities when a thunderstorm struck a local dwelling nearby. These thunderstorms were as furious as they were sudden; they came out of nowhere on a bright sunny day, wreaked havoc and vanished as quickly as they appeared. This one struck fast and struck hard near the village where the local shepherds had built a crude but effective dam which held a strong and powerful stream at bay. Five seconds of persistent lightning bolts passing anywhere between a million and one billion volts of pure electricity and the dam was decimated.

The raging water spilt over and washed off half the village. Most villagers escaped the fury of the unleashed water but a few were trapped standing on top of their unstable and fragile shelters. It would be days before any administrative aid could reach such a disconnected area. The young soldiers of the Punjab Regiment rose to the occasion and went off to help, leaving only skeletal staff manning Ring Contour.

An alert and watchful enemy saw the opportunity and seized it; their attack was swift and merciless. The few soldiers of the Punjab Regiment manning Ring Contour fought back but they stood no chance, they were completely outnumbered. The enemy took no prisoners and allowed no one to escape.

All the Indians were killed and their bodies were thrown off the cliff face. With this sudden and very successful attack, the enemy had now taken complete control over Ring Contour.

There were several logistical nightmares to be dealt with. At nine thousand feet with unpredictable weather and limited visibility, the air force wouldn't be of much help. With crevices, caves and contours, heavy artillery and missiles too would have limited effect. For recapture and occupation, there was no alternative for sending soldiers in who would have to climb and fight their way through every inch of the tricky topography.

This inevitability of harsh man to man combat settled on Colonel Dragon, Commanding Officer of the Punjabis… he understood that a lot of blood was going to be spilt in the very near future and much of that blood would be of his own men.

He had gone through 'Sitreps' from all his forward posts and it was time for him to send his 'Sitrep' to his boss."

"What's a Sitrep?" Ashiana Mehta asked.

Brij turned around and replied before Indu could. He said, "That's military jargon for Situation Report. In field areas, Sitreps are sent upwards and downwards the chain of command to keep everyone up to speed on the latest happenings because along the Line of Control combat situations are fluid and dynamic, they keep changing in hours and minutes."

"Very good Brij!" Indu remarked, visibly impressed.

Brij was taken aback that she knew his name but he loved the appreciation. "Thank you Ma'am, I read a lot."

Indu continued, "The Sitreps confirmed that the enemy had completely occupied Ring Contour and commanded a tactical view over movements made far within the Indian dominion. Col Dragon grieved for those of his soldiers who had already been killed in the vicious enemy attack. Anyone in his battalion was family; he felt he had lost his own children.

His head spun and he felt nauseous but Dragon's face betrayed none of this turmoil except for his bloodshot eyes which gave away the fact that he hadn't slept at all. 'Focus,' he said to himself, he needed to evict the enemy immediately with minimum losses.

Dragon had worked round the clock for the last seventy two hours. The first need was several detailed briefings followed by visits to the closest points from where he could see the occupied locations, understand and assess the situation. He then planned a counterattack with his core team to regain their lost land while, at the same time, ensuring minimum casualties.

The windowless Ops room in which he sat was brightly lit, there were several maps all over the walls; a few monitors displayed the latest satellite photographs that had come in a few minutes ago. In the middle of the Ops room was a large three-dimensional model of the entire conflict zone replicating every detail exactly as it really was.

As battalion commander, Dragon had four companies under his command. Each one had about a hundred and fifty soldiers and was headed by a Major who was seconded by a Captain or a Lieutenant. These companies were named Alfa, Bravo, Charlie and Delta.

All four company commanders had volunteered and wanted to spearhead the mission but Dragon selected and put Major Baaz of Charlie Company in charge. Though the others were extremely competent and dependable, Baaz was by far the best bet Dragon had and he wasn't willing to take any chances.

Baaz had a sterling record of service and military lineage that made him infallible. Besides, the troops worshiped him and would happily follow him into hell and back if required. They trusted him completely.

Major Baaz was as good as nobility in his hometown because he came from a family of wealthy landlords that owned large tracts of land spread across acres and acres of beautiful mountains in a state called Himachal Pradesh in the North of India where it was a tradition that every family contributed one male member to the Army, Navy or Air Force as a service to the nation, an honour normally accorded to the eldest offspring.

Baaz was the third male child; his father had decided that the eldest son would apply for Officer Training in the Army. His second son would watch over the farm lands and Baaz being the third would be sent abroad to pursue further studies, then return to implement his knowledge in their hometown to improve the quality of life and output of the entire village.

Young Baaz had other plans for himself; he was obsessed with joining the Army. Once he got to know of his father's designs, he decided to short-circuit the entire plan. He didn't wait for graduation or even to finish his studies. On his 18th birthday, he landed at the local recruitment office and got himself enlisted as a soldier.

His elder brother was of course sent for further studies to the U.K. Baaz meanwhile served in the toughest battle-infested zones of India and displayed the highest quality of leadership. With sheer grit and performance, he worked his way up to becoming a commissioned officer. He topped his batch with the best scores and highest honours; he had even been awarded a 'Kirti Chakra' - the second highest medal for bravery for his valour in combat.

His style was unique in that, his eyes were perpetually half closed and he appeared to be dozing and stationery but when he moved, he moved suddenly with unnatural speed and accuracy. His style was like a hawk that lazily circles the skies high up above and appears unaware of the world below. However, it has actually already spotted and homed in on its prey. Then without warning, it suddenly swoops down and grabs its prey which rarely stands a chance and before you know it, it is back in the skies, too high and too far to catch. It was this similarity in style which earned him the nickname Baaz which means hawk in English. He loved sports and good food. Tandoori chicken and butter naans were his favourites;

he could never have enough of them and it was beginning to show too! Having been an enlisted soldier himself, his rapport with his troops was like that of a father with his children. Soldiers doted on him and almost everyone wanted to be under his command.

Col Dragon said, "Gentlemen, we've sorted out all loose ends, this operation will be called 'Operation Kirpan'."

"Wait a minute...," Ishra interrupted Indu, ... "What's *kirpan*?"

Indu responded, "Col Dragon had thought this through very carefully. He wanted a name that would represent what they were going to fight and possibly die for. He needed every soldier in his unit to understand the importance of this operation and there was no name better than *kirpan*.

A *kirpan* is a curved knife or blade carried by Sikhs. In 1699, Guru Gobind Singh told his Sikhs to wear a *kirpan* at all times in order to protect the weak from tyranny and slavery, to maintain a state of harmony and security, to allow for the development of trade, craftsmanship and literature and to safeguard the universal right of all beings to live their lives in a peaceful, stable and sheltered environment.

The word *kirpan* has two roots – the first root is: *kirpa* which means 'Mercy, grace, compassion, kindness' and the second root is *aan* which in turn means 'Honour, grace, dignity.' So together the word stands for 'the dignity and honour of compassion, kindness and mercy.'

Symbolically, the *kirpan* represents the power of truth to cut through untruth. It is the cutting edge of the enlightened mind. The bearer of a *kirpan* has left behind a life of subservience and is duty bound to protect justice for all the people of the world; to side with the oppressed and support all weaker inhabitants without any reference to their race, gender, caste, nationality, religion or beliefs.

Coming back to our story, Col Dragon presented a background and then called Baaz forward.

"Baaz, let's begin your briefing."

Baaz was in front of the sand model in a flash. He held a six-foot-long wooden pointer in his hand and commenced.

"The objective of Operation Kirpan is to regain and permanently hold Ring Contour.

Let me start with a description of Ring Contour. It is an isolated monolithic hill feature, the tallest in the vicinity and is situated on the LOC. The climb upward is almost vertical except for two rungs in between and it peaks with a helmet-like top.

The enemy has occupied all levels of Ring Contour and therefore holds complete tactical advantage. Ideally, I would have liked the Air Force to have bombed him senseless before our ground assault but since the weather doesn't permit, we'll rely on heavy artillery, missile and mortar fire to disorient him. They will blast all enemy positions with everything they have and their fire will lift only when we are fifty meters short of the enemy.

The enemy holds the dominating positions and knows we are coming for him; the only factor in our favour is the precise time of the assault which will give us a momentary advantage of surprise. No beating around the bush, ours will be a direct full frontal assault.

Op Kirpan will be executed in three phases as follows:

PHASE 1:

Our first phase will begin from the point still held by us closest to Ring Contour and then climb up the slopes; these slopes have gradients of about 30 to 45 degrees and then flatten out after about a hundred meters to form the first rung of defense. When last held by us, this rung was populated with nine bunkers. By the time we capture, sanitize and occupy these bunkers, hours of darkness will be getting over. We will use the next day's light to consolidate our positions and establish an axis of maintenance from base till the first rung. This axis will help us remove our dead, wounded and bring in fresh supplies, troops and medical aid.

First and second platoons of Charlie Company will spearhead this assault. Third Platoon Charlie Company and First Platoon Delta Company will be following and providing all support required.

PHASE 2:

First and second Platoons of Charlie Company that

spearheaded the assault in Phase 1 will dig and stay put. Their back up that was Third Platoon Charlie Company and First Platoon Delta Company will now spearhead Phase 2. Their back up will be Second and Third Platoons of Delta Company.

We launch Phase 2 again at night under the cover of darkness from our new base - the first rung of Ring Contour. Again our assault will be preceded by heavy artillery, missile and mortar fire on the enemy to have him disoriented by the time we get to him. After a little flat ground the upward slopes start again, starting at forty five degrees and moving to sixty and seventy degree gradients. The terrain is undulating, full of loose gravel stones and lots of crevices; it flattens out again in another eighty meters to form the second rung which will be Phase 2 of Operation Kirpan. Last known, we had five bunkers here. Complete reoccupation of all bunkers in this rung is our objective in Phase 2.

This Phase will be much tougher because we would have completely lost the element of surprise and the slopes are much steeper here. Our own troops will also be fatigued by this time. The assaulting platoons will dig in and stay put. Once again, we will use the following daylight to bring up our axis of maintenance to our forward most point.

Our three phases span three nights and two days. We will attack by night and use the daytime for moving our wounded, dead, getting spares, weapons, ammunition, food, water, equipment, etc. but please remember that the enemy holds the high ground and that makes us sitting ducks in a shooting gallery during the daylight. Hence, all movement will have to be hunkered down and with great caution.

PHASE 3:

We will commence this Phase on the third night of our Op Kirpan. Second and Third platoons of Delta Company will spearhead this attack and we will launch from the second rung of Ring Contour. Fresh troops of Alpha Company who would have sneaked in during the day will be the backup this time. Also fresh troops of Bravo Company would have moved in and relieved our battle-worn troops holding the first two rungs of Ring Contour.

Thirty meters of flat stretch and the gradient starts with sixty degree slopes, occasionally going to ninety degrees with a few over hangs as well. It is an exhausting and a treacherous climb. Eighty meters upward is the final helmet-shaped top of Ring Contour which will be phase three...the final phase of Operation Kirpan. This area is capricious so it poses dangers to us, yet the rock formations provide natural fortifications to the enemy troops. The helmet-shaped top is about four hundred and fifty meters in diameter and sprinkled with bunkers three hundred and sixty degrees around. The command bunker is at its pinnacle.

Phase 3 will be the toughest of the lot because the enemy will have nowhere to run; they will fight to the last man and with several advantages on their side because by then we will have very few hours of cover of darkness left. Our troops will also be mentally and physically exhausted by then and the enemy dominates most paths leading to the top."

"Party of the year, count me in!" Major Green commented.

Baaz paused, then pointed to specific markings at the top of Ring Contour in his model and said, "We have sent a few recce patrols that have made feint attacks and tricked the enemy into revealing his gun nests. They are here, here and here. Based on this info we have managed to chalk out a route plan which should give us maximum cover. We will of course still have causalities but we will make it to the op and reclaim Ring Contour completely.

Lt. Col Wolf was the second in charge after Dragon, the wellbeing of troops was his direct responsibility. He carefully contemplated the situation before he spoke. "Tired and exhausted troops, no element of surprise, fighting upslope against a dominating and prepared enemy who, in the absence of a place to retreat, will fight with all they have: all of this sounds very tough Baaz. Very, very tough. Where will you be through all of this? And what's your chain of command?"

"I will be up in front leading the assault in all 3 phases with my men Sir. Delta Company Commander Green will be my second in command. Captain Ice will handle our frontline logistics, support fire and be our next in hierarchy. After him will be Manny.

In each phase, Manny will be with me all the time in every assault. Once we breach the enemy's perimeter, Green and Ice will tailgate and slingshot their teams to the left and right respectively, assaulting the enemy from within their own flanks.

A seasoned soldier himself and an old friend of Baaz, Lt. Col Wolf looked at Maj Green who was immersed in the discussion. He knew Green well and had great respect for him. Like Baaz, Green too was a combat veteran who was well-known for his infectious energy and his ability to motivate troops. Wolf then turned his head back to see Captain Ice who sat stretched out in a chair. His eyes were covered by his combat hat. He saw Wolf turn around and doffed his hat mildly in response. 'I wonder if his is a case of all show and no go,' Wolf thought to himself. He wasn't comfortable with Ice for several reasons. Ice had joined the unit recently from his Sri Lankan tenure and didn't know all the troops personally. So he had yet to earn his respect and establish his place among them. Besides, Ice was from the 'Specfore' (Special Forces). Wolf had encountered his kind before. They were normally mavericks and unpredictable wildcards…no one could say what they would do next or what they were capable of. Ice was a Kavvach operative, that made him a shade wilder than the usual Specfore types. Wolf didn't like unpredictability; he was a disciplinarian who felt secure within systems and templates.

Ice's battle record was like a white paper on combat but Wolf still had his apprehensions. Fighting guerillas in dense jungles was very different from a head-on assault on trained regular army soldiers in the mountains. The enemy and the terrain varied.

Jungles had thick air heavy with moisture while air in the mountains was thin. Besides, running up and down mountains was tough. While jungles had swamps, mountains had a treacherous topography. Even the basic rules of colour and camouflage differed between the two. That wasn't all, even food, water and method of movements differed greatly between the two.

Guerillas were normally highly motivated but they were underequipped and worked with makeshift arrangements. They specialized in ambushes and booby traps while regular army soldiers were well-trained, properly equipped and had strong support systems.

Ice would have to face many challenges, both internal and external to be successful here.

"Where's Manny?" Wolf asked.

Baaz replied, "He is already at the forward fire base sir, firming up our assault logistics and troops sir. He's also looking into details like blackening and dulling all metal parts so that no one gets seen by reflecting light and ensuring that every man in the assault team carries the right gear."

With over twenty five years of service and nine medals earned in the most hazardous terrains known to man, Sergeant Major Manvinder Singh, known to all as Manny, was as reliable as the sunrise.

5

What kind of names are these?" Brij asked. It doesn't sound like the Indian Army to me. We don't have names like Dragon, Wolf, Green, Ice or Baaz."

"True…" Indu said, "…very true Brij, the Indian Army was originally raised by the British when they ruled India and they put regiments together based on communities, states and castes. So we have regiments called Punjab, Sikh, Madras, Rajput, Marathas, Dogras and many more, all based on caste. The Army still follows many traditions but it also does experiment, adapt and evolve all the time and that's probably why it is such a successful one. We have one of the finest combat records in the world.

Dragon's boss Brigadier Sher Ali Khan was an outstanding General reputed for his vision and intelligence who had fought gallantly in the 1965 and 1971 wars and was a proud patriot. He identified an enemy with the potential to tear our country apart and fragment it worse than any external aggressor could. This disturbed him greatly and he had to do something about it."

"Who was this enemy?" Kiran Bawa asked.

Indu carried on, "Over the years, he had witnessed several communal conflicts. Inter-religious riots and violence took place occasionally; less written about was intra-religious caste-based divides and atrocities that took place across the country. These ranged from labelling and passing snide remarks and went on up to extreme inhuman violence, for example, a Dalit would get his legs chopped off if he walked through the property that belonged to a person above his caste. Such occurrences mortified Sher Ali Khan and disturbed him greatly."

Brij said "I've read about such savage incidents in our history books."

Indu responded, "Such heinous acts of villainy continue in pockets even now Brij. As recently as February 2012, a Dalit man's arm was chopped off for drinking water from the pot of an upper caste person in Hisar district of Haryana.

Sher Ali Khan noted that Indians are born and bred in highly communal environments. Caste consciousness is inculcated in most Indians at a very young age and since the Army draws its resources from the masses, it was impossible to prevent such divides and awareness from creeping into the system. He believed that naming regiments after communities and states only heightened this potential weakness. An army infiltrated by caste and communalism couldn't possibly be at its best. This was a crack that needed to be plugged before the entire dam burst.

However, there was little he could do about restructuring the entire Indian Army at that point. For that, he'd have to wait until, one day, he became the Chief of Army Staff. Till then, he'd have to tackle this issue in his own way with the resources under his command. He preferred officers from communities different from the men they led, that minimized labelling and over-familiarity. This however, was also not always possible.

So Brigadier Sher Ali Khan designed an ingenious way to mask all religious, and caste-based identities. All officers in his command were given nicknames by which they would be officially addressed. These nicknames were earned and awarded by the consensus of the individual and all unit hands together. Names had to be such that they would not give away caste or religion and would be used to address the officer at all times. It protected them and their families during sensitive operations."

"Colonel Dragon is an intriguing name. Why was he called that?" Kim asked.

Indu pleasantly said, "Because he was known for his wisdom and effervescent temper. They say he spewed fire when he was angry."

"And Green and Ice?" Kiran asked.

"Patience, I'll get to each one as we go along," Indu said, "Unlike Baaz's ancestry, Captain Ice was a city boy with no military lineage; nobody from his family had been in the Army. Born and brought up in an upmarket area of what was then called Bombay, his natural language was English and he dressed casually unlike most Army officers. His overall military etiquette was quite poor."

"You mean he was badly brought up?" Ashiana asked, wide eyed.

Indu continued, "Differently brought up. He wouldn't get up every time a senior officer entered the room and wouldn't end his meal the minute his senior did. He encouraged his subordinates to 'chill' in his presence and didn't understand why it was so important to change into a dining uniform to have dinner every night. Sycophancy was beyond him; he encouraged questions and would freely question superiors much to their astonishment since they were not used to the idea of teaming up with such a person.

His poor command over Hindi and Punjabi, languages spoken by the soldiers, lack of military manners, disinterest in internal power play or politics, fondness for pop music in general, rock bands such as GnR and Deep Purple being his favourites set him apart from all the rest. Some found it hard to identify with him and yet these very qualities gave him an endearing affability because of which his popularity soared. He wasn't competition to anyone. Officers and soldiers alike loved being in his company because they found him a loveable conundrum that was completely dependable yet far removed from their local issues."

"So he was he called Ice because he was a cool dude?" Kim asked.

Indu continued, "In the battlefield another side of him came alive. He moved like lightning, his slim, wiry and lean frame could jump over anything. He was the fastest in his batch in tackling obstacle courses. He ran five kilometers in nineteen minutes with combat equipment and was a marksman who never missed.

When he graduated as a commissioned officer, Ice posted a request for the Specfore. His request was granted and he was put in the probation programme considered one of the toughest in the world. His exemplary performance grabbed the attention of a few higher ups in the elite forces and he was offered a spot in the much-coveted Kavvach commando unit.

Kavvach units comprised small teams of handpicked men from the Specfore; they specialized in deep penetration ops within enemy territory. They were like phantoms, considered the best of the best. They were outside the normal military hierarchy and were answerable only to the Chief of Army Staff.

Twenty-two-year-old Ice was airdropped after a rocky ride into the heart of a hot battle zone amidst heavy enemy fire. After he landed, he had to help load corpses of Indian soldiers back into the same transport. His spanking new uniform was instantly blood-soaked. If that wasn't bad enough, the very chopper he had landed in and helped load was blown out of the sky seconds after takeoff by the LTTE's deadly missiles. The explosion rained blood and body parts of the same dead soldiers he had just helped load.

His Kavvach unit was inserted in the heart of enemy territory to sniff out hidden camps that held Indian soldiers prisoner within dense jungles and get them back alive. These were dangerous missions and it is said that Kavvach teams wouldn't brush their teeth, have bath or even eat cooked food for two entire weeks before each insertion so that they could become one with the jungle. Then neither man, animal, reptile or insect could smell or detect them. They were self-sufficient in every way and vanished for months together; they smelled, looked and moved like the forest itself; they were ghosts who were feared by beast and man alike.

On his very first such operation, two of his senior officers were killed and Ice found himself commanding war-hardened soldiers through intense fire surrounded by the enemy. Ice stayed cool, never panicked and was the most prudent and patient officer anyone had ever come across. He earned his first medal for bringing his entire team back home alive and successfully rescuing seventeen Indian soldiers who were being held by the enemy. What came out as his outstanding feature was his incredible ability to stay completely calm and composed even in the worst situations. They said he had no blood, only ice in his veins.

His tactics were bold and unpredictable and he maintained an enviable combat folio. His performance ensured that he was awarded a 'Chief of Army Staff Commendation Card' along with an out-of-turn promotion. He made it to Lieutenant within three months and in less than a year, he was again promoted; this time to Captain. By the time the Indian

Army pulled out of Sri Lanka, Ice was hardly twenty three years old but had two medals for his intrepid conduct and held the record for most successful commando raids inside enemy territory with minimum loss of life.

He never hesitated before pulling the trigger of his weapon, there was never any hint of emotion on his face. His nerves of steel and cool demeanor made him the perfect hunter and earned him the nickname 'Ice'."

"Wow!" Sandy said, "What a personality! At twenty two, most guys here check out nightclubs, cars, phones and women."

"Yes!" Indu responded. "Ice was from a well-off family, he could have simply joined his father's business or studied further but he felt a greater calling. He craved to serve his motherland the best way he could so was by applying for and getting into the army."

"Wow!" Sandy said again, "That's passion!"

"So how did he land in the Punjab Regiment from the Specfore?" Brij asked.

Indu replied, "When the Indian Army pulled out of Sri Lanka after years of battle, Kavvach units were also pulled out. Since they had seen the worst of action for years there, their team members were sent temporarily to non-Specfore units for a two-year breather. So Ice found himself in this

Punjab unit. It had only been over a month and he was still new to the men, which was one more reason why Wolf had his doubts about Ice.

Discussions and detailing in Dragon's Ops room went on for long as they ironed out wrinkles on weaponry, timings, support teams, communications, loads, command centers and many other battle details. At 1800h, that is 6pm, Baaz, Green and Ice exited Dragon's Ops room and headed straight for the frontlines.

'Operation Kirpan' had already kicked off; the Line of Control was abuzz with activity. On Dragon's instructions, several other units had begun moving in their 81 millimeter mortars, Milan missiles and heavy machine gun teams into the area to take positions on the Indian side. These teams would hammer the enemy and soften them up for Baaz's assault teams.

Baaz, Green and Ice reached Tindi and without wasting a moment, began their march downward towards the combat zone. It was two hours of hard trek away but the thumps were already loud and clear. Forty five minutes later, Baaz and his team came into full view of the combat zone. Streams of white dashes from either side crisscrossed the sky. Tracer rounds lit up the night. Regular mortar shelling sounds overlapped with sounds of heavy machine gun fire and the occasional single rifle shots too. The whining sounds of shrapnel ricocheting off metal and flying freely skywards couldn't be missed.

Baaz switched on his PNVD (Passive Night Vision Device) glasses; the screen flickered on and in a scratchy green colour he watched two Indian soldiers crawl towards a vantage point with a shoulder-fired rocket launcher. He panned his glasses to the left and could clearly see three enemy soldiers manning a medium gun overlooking the two Indians... they hadn't seen the Indians yet. Baaz knew that the moment the Indians opened fire, they'd be spotted by the machine gun crew and they'd be perforated. With no direct communication to them, there was nothing he could do so he flicked the power switch off and muttered, "We'd better get down there fast." They resumed their climb downwards. The night lit up for a brief moment as the two soldiers let loose a rocket at an enemy position, it hit home killing a few but they didn't live to see it as the enemy's medium machine gun crew spotted and opened fire on them within seconds of their position being revealed. They died instantly.

After a long and arduous trek, they finally reached the staging area that was bustling with activity and sneaked into a makeshift bunker where they were greeted and briefed by a greatly relieved Sergeant Major Manny. He first saluted Baaz sharply with a crisp "Jai Hind". When Baaz returned his salute, Manny spoke "We've been waiting for your return. What are your orders Sir?"

Baaz said, "First synchronize watches with me, get all platoon and section heads here in five minutes but before that, send me my Sahayak."

Though India gained its freedom in 1947, several systems, procedures and traditions laid down by the British continued and were still followed religiously. Every officer was assigned an administrative helper called a 'Sahayak, Batman or Orderly'. The Sahayak would do everything from serving bed tea in the morning to polishing shoes and helping out in household chores like grocery shopping, chopping vegetables and dropping the officer's children to school.

The Sahayak was a combat soldier who was invariably well-mannered and docile as no officer would want a hot-blooded warrior in his home with his wife and children. These Sahayaks also enjoyed a few privileges like getting the best of equipment and rations and occasionally being excused from soldierly duties like early morning physical exercises, sentry duty, Battle Physical Efficiency Tests and target practice. This wasn't a written rule; it was a culture that had set in, an unspoken norm...the battle-worthiness of a Sahayak was rarely questioned.

Baaz's Sahayak Shaitan Singh scurried into the makeshift bunker. He carried with him a cross strap fixed to a combat web belt along with an assault rifle and an automatic pistol. Baaz held out his arms to his sides as Shaitan Singh strapped the equipment expertly... he had done this a million times before. The web belt had ten grenades already primed and kept in its pouches. He then brought out six sets of fully loaded magazines; each set had two inverted magazines taped to each other. This would help changing magazines quickly in the heat of battle where every second counted. Without wasting a moment, he attached another two pouches full of ammunition to the web belt and a third with six magazines filled for the pistol. Last of all, he attached a water bottle and then stood three feet away opposite Baaz.

Manny entered the bunker again with the NCOs and Baaz began briefing them. They listened carefully and interrupted with questions rarely. Once the briefing was done and all questions answered, the team rushed out to brief the rest of the troops.

Shaitan Singh stood by even after everyone left, he seemed tentative about something. "What is it?" Baaz asked. Shaitan Singh hesitated and spoke, "Sir, may I come along?" Baaz didn't respond immediately. When he finally spoke, his tone was benign. "How long have you been a Sahayak for?" Shaitan Singh responded quickly, "Nine years sir." Baaz's next question was quick, "When did you last attend physical training?" Shaitan hesitated, "I don't know." Baaz's final question was "When did you last fire a weapon?" Shaitan Singh was again completely lost. After a lot of thought, he said, "Maybe a year back."

Baaz continued, "Shaitan..." he said, "...for the last nine years you have taken care of my family and me. You have spared no effort and untiringly given us your best. Today it's finally my turn to take care of you so listen to me carefully, this operation is nothing like the ones we've done before. These aren't half-witted militants or desperate terrorists. These are highly motivated, well-trained and well-equipped soldiers of the regular army and they hold every tactical advantage over us. This is going to be one of the toughest combat situations possible. If you were better trained I'd definitely take you along but right now with your current level of preparedness, your best chances of staying alive are as far away from this combat zone as possible and that's exactly where I am going to keep you."

Baaz knew that Shaitan Singh's request was genuine and he wouldn't be afraid in the face of gunfire but he was uncertain about Shaitan Singh's ability to take another human's life. Shaitan Singh simply didn't have the 'Look'. The 'Look' as it is often referred to in military and police circles is one which sets in after years of exposure to extreme violence. It is an unflinching, weather-beaten, detached, confident and hardened look that most hard-boiled soldiers acquire after tough service on the battlefront. The look is what the police and security agencies often watch out for in airports or at other checkpoints. It is also what makes battle veterans stand apart from civilians even after they leave service.

The Look can't be acquired by making a face or faking a pose. It isn't taught in military manuals but is acquired after prolonged exposure to combat. While most Hollywood films are extremely accurate in replicating weapons, equipment and battle scenes, they still often fall short of reality because of the inability to get adequate actors with the 'Look'.

Shaitan Singh was crestfallen but he knew better than to argue with Baaz so he stood aside silently. Baaz looked affectionately at him. Shaitan Singh was five feet nine inches tall but years of humble service had made him hunch a little. His wide and kind eyes looked down and his pockmark ridden face appeared sad. The role of Sahayak fitted him perfectly. When Baaz's family joined him, Shaitan Singh was the family favourite. Baaz knew that this was the best decision; it would save Shaitan Singh and help keep the assaulting force lethal and deadly.

Manny was a personification of the 'Look'. His turban, moustache and beard covered most of his face but his eyes were inescapable. When he looked at people, they usually gave him their complete attention. His chiseled face had lines etched across it, the furrows on his forehead seemed as if someone had carved them with a knife. His dented cheeks and highlighted cheekbones made him extremely good-looking in a rugged John Wayne sort of way. Manny was a veteran of many battles. After twenty years in the Army as a fighting soldier, he had earned enough medals to make his uniform look like a mosaic but that was a small part of him. Sergeant Major Manny was a warrior by heritage and one of the finest at that. His lineage went back by three hundred years because he was a thoroughbred Nihang.

A Nihang is a Saint-Warrior. The very mention of 'Nihangs' used to strike fear in the hearts of Mughals over three hundred years ago. Since then, the Nihangs have managed to retain their sanctity.

Nihang is the Persian word for crocodile and that's how the terrified Mughals described their fighting style. Also known as Akalis, the Nihang is an order of the Sikh community that does not fear death, is beyond material possessions and exists only to do its duty. The term 'Akali' is derived from the Punjabi term *Akal Purukh* which means 'the Timeless One' (God). 'Akali' therefore means 'Servitor of the Timeless God'.

They wear dark blue robes with their legs bare below the knees and blue and yellow turbans laced with steel discs. They usually carry spears, swords, daggers and shields.

It is said that the order was founded more than three hundred years ago by Guru Gobind Singhji himself as the fighting body of the Khalsa. He said that the Nihangs will be generous and follow strict adherence to *dharma*. When a Nihang wields his sword, it will give out sparks like fireworks. Renowned for their martial skills, the Nihangs are the vanguards of Sikhs, whose vocation in life is to be a warrior, protect and be at the forefront of battles.

Sikh history is populated with stories of the courage of the Akali order. The Akalis are known for their valour and their ability to hold on even when heavily outnumbered.

Manny could be in his Indian Army combat fatigues, a tuxedo or even dressed as an astronaut; it didn't matter because there was no softening of his look or the kind of fear his gaze invoked. He followed Baaz and they slipped out of the bunker ready for battle.

6

0200H: 23ND AUGUST 1991

Major Baaz and his men crouched behind a small fold in the ground barely fifty meters from the enemy positions. He looked at his watch. He knew that supporting fire would commence in exactly three minutes. He suppressed a sudden craving for tandoori chicken with butter naan, closed his eyes and took a few slow and deep breaths.

Exactly one hundred and eighty seconds later, the entire Indian side of Ring Contour came alive with a thunderstorm of heavy fire. As per Dragon's plan, two artillery units stationed three kilometers away, six mortar teams, twelve heavy machine gun teams and two wire-guided missile teams opened fire on the enemy at the same time. Baaz and his men couldn't stop themselves from peeking to see what was happening to their enemy. Clouds of smoke rose as the deafening roar of manmade thunder continued. The enemy was being pulverized too severely to be able to spot the Indian infantrymen creeping in, they moved as close as they could without being hit by friendly fire.

Manny was next to Baaz right at the front of the assault line. Without taking his eyes off the enemy, his right hand reached down and touched the earth. He took a little gravel in his hand, rubbed it across his forehead and mumbled to himself in his native Punjabi, "*Maa tusi fikar na kar, mein tere lai aariya.*" That meant, 'Mother, don't worry. I am coming for you.'

Baaz wordlessly signalled his troops to be ready, then picked up the handset of the radio and spoke one word into it: "Zeba." Then, he waited.

Sixty seconds later the Indian barrage at the base of Ring Contour ceased. For a brief while, an ominous silence hung in the air. Then, without warning, Baaz and his men sprang out and charged full front at the enemy.

The merciless battering had taken its toll on the enemy. When it stopped, many were dead; survivors were wounded or deaf, the insides of their bunkers were scattered with body parts, broken weapons and splotches of crimson everywhere. The air was heavy with debris and dust. They barely managed to catch their breath when sheer dread overcame them. They knew this respite was the uneasy calm that comes before a torrid storm. They quickly gathered what was left of their wits and manned their positions. They looked out but couldn't see anything till the air cleared a little and visibility improved, the sight they saw then curdled their blood.

Dauntless soldiers of Charlie Company led by Major Baaz tore into the enemy's perimeter with superhuman ruthlessness. Battle cries rang in the air as the enemy opened up with everything they had but the heroic Punjabis and their mad officers didn't relent. They ran right up to the enemy positions and flung grenades into their bunkers before standing aside. As the grenades went off, the Punjabis charged into the bunkers, firing accurately.

This battle was of the toughest kind; it was bestial man to man combat. Rifle butts, bayonets and grenades were used freely. No quarter was asked for and none was given. The enemy fought back to the best of their ability but they were no match for Charlie Company.

Green and Ice's teams wasted no time; they caught up with Baaz's frontline then fanned out and launched an assault towards the left and right flanks. The confused enemy didn't expect to be fired at from their own flanks. They didn't put up too much of a fight and began to desert their positions after offering a token resistance.

Ninety seven minutes later, a blackened, out-of-breath, bruised yet composed Major Baaz spoke into the handset of his radio set. This time too it was one word. "Peter".

Colonel Dragon listened motionlessly to every sound that was made and every word that was spoken throughout the attack. When he finally heard 'Peter,' he exulted, "Baaz has done it! The maniac has actually done it. Phase 1 is a resounding success. One down, two to go!"

Fifteen minutes later, Baaz's latest sitrep was handed over to Dragon. He read it out aloud, "Baaz's gathering forces for Phase 2. Make sure he has all the support he needs. Get the wounded and dead out of there first." Wolf saluted smartly and turned away to execute Dragon's instructions.

0730H - 1700H, 23RD AUGUST 1991

It was daylight now. The enemy kept up the pressure by firing without a break but Baaz and his boys were well dug in. There wasn't much to do except lying low and waiting for the night.

Movement was minimal as visibility was greater in broad daylight and anything that was seen was shot instantly. For both sides the rule was simple. When in doubt, shoot to kill. Despite this, every fold in the ground was used as cover and like master craftsmen at work, Indians stealthily evacuated their wounded and brought in fresh troops to fill the void. Food, water, ammunition, spares, equipment, etc also seeped in silently to the frontlines.

1745H 23RD AUGUST 1991

Darkness began to creep in and both sides were preparing for another night of mayhem. Ice looked at Manny and asked, "Is it me or is it really getting colder?" Manny looked around and responded, "Yes sir, it is getting colder. In fact I think it may start snowing soon."

Baaz moved deftly along the mountainside. He was careful not to be seen by the enemy. He made it a point to visit each and every one of his soldiers at least three times during the day. Morale was high amongst the men, the previous night's success had them itching for more. Medical aid, fresh ammunition, weapons and other equipment had reached them. The dead and wounded had been cleared. They couldn't wait for nightfall to get back into action again.

Baaz made his way back to his command position; they had

taken back the complete bottom rung of Ring Contour, had scaled maybe forty percent of the sides and thus driven a wedge into enemy-occupied land. Baaz knew that the previous night's assault was by far the easiest. From now on, it would get progressively tougher. Firstly, they'd be going uphill against an enemy that held all the high ground. Secondly, surprise was now lost because earlier, while the enemy knew that they would strike, they didn't know exactly when. Thirdly, now that they were at such close proximity to the enemy that getting artillery and mortar support would be very difficult. Lastly, regardless of morale, the troops would be tiring out soon.

Phase 2 was set to kick off at 2323h that night.

Ice had made full use of the daytime lull in the battle. He had taken charge of the staging area and ensured that a logistical axis of maintenance was open from the Indian side right up to the frontline. This included ammunition, weaponry, medical aid, casualty evacuation processes. He had also established a wired telephone line from base right up to Baaz. This guaranteed secure and safe communication directly between Major Baaz and Colonel Dragon.

Simple though this may sound, it was extremely difficult because daylight exposed all Indian movements and the enemy's height afforded them direct dominance over the conflict zone.

Ice came up with an ingenious idea. He requested Colonel Dragon for fifty teams of snipers to be placed around Ring

Contour, covering it from top to bottom with distinct areas of responsibility earmarked for each sniper team.

Dragon turned to Brigadier Sher Ali Khan who approved instantly. Fifty of the best snipers were put together from various battalions across the brigade. Each sniper team had two men, one was the main sniper with the rifle and the other was his spotter. Every sniper team was given two sniper rifles with ten thousand rounds of sniper ammo, bipods, personal weapons with separate ammunition, a telephone line, a radio set with five spare batteries, food, water, binoculars, spare telescopes, hunting daggers and bayonets.

The sniper teams trickled in throughout the day and Ice kept positioning them at various strategic locations. He gave each team a number and clear instructions, "Dig in, camouflage yourself and your muzzle flash completely; cover your designated zones effectively, keep communication lines open but use the wired lines since they are secure. If they fail then and only then use the wireless radio, that too as per the encryptions provided. No smoking, no coughing, no noise at all."

At 2030h, Manny snuck in behind a fold in the ground. It was a cold night and his joints were getting stiff. He tried to stretch his arms and legs without having them shot at by the ever-vigilant enemy. Havildar (Sergeant) Ram Singh was next to him. Ram Singh's nose and eyes wrinkled as he looked at Manny with a toothy grin. They had joined the army together over two decades ago, now they were both above forty years old.

They were the best of friends but Ram Singh and Manny were as different as chalk and cheese. Manny was physically very fit, polished, suave and understated. Ram Singh looked like a typical Indian farmer. Blunt in his thoughts and actions, his teeth were stained. He loved his *chai*, enjoyed smoking *bidis*, threw temper tantrums and his uniform was shabby. If Manny was allowed to choose who he could share this 'fox hole' with, he'd pick Ram Singh without a thought because Ram Singh was a brilliant soldier who took and executed orders without exception. Had he been a little more polished and well turned out, he too would have made it to Manny's rank by now.

Ram Singh broke the silence, "So here we are again my brother. How many times have we been like this before?" Manny sighed, "Too many times my friend, too many times." Manny was going to say something more but the expression on Ram Singh's face made him stop. Ram Singh was straining to listen to something, Manny's senses immediately heightened and he went into a state of complete alertness.

Ram Singh's blackened, crooked finger pointed towards the sky. Then he quickly signalled his men to take cover. Manny heard a sound in the air. It was a whining kind of noise that seemed to be getting louder. This was a sound he had heard a million times before but it seemed to be headed straight at him. He shrunk to make himself as tiny as possible. Ram Singh was gesturing wildly at his men who cringed behind every little bit of shelter but overhead cover was almost nonexistent. There was a bright blinding flash a few feet away from Manny and he felt like he was hit by a truck, he felt himself haplessly fly in the air like a weightless blade of grass and hit the ground on his back with a thump. The back of his head followed with a whack but was protected by his combat helmet. And, there was momentary darkness.

When he opened his eyes, his vision was blurred. All he could hear were sounds like those made by high speed howling winds. He wiped his eyes on the sleeve of his tunic and looked down at himself in the haze of the dark night sky. Ram Singh appeared close in front of him, saying something. Manny stared back blankly. He still couldn't hear well. Ram Singh propped him up against a large rock that protected them from direct enemy fire. Manny managed to look left. He saw a pitch black crater in the mountain face exactly where some of Ram Singh's men had been a few seconds ago. Now there was no one there, just a few limbs, weapons and other broken equipment.

Baaz picked up his phone; it was a small green rectangular box. A spiral telephone cord that led to a handset came out of one end and the other end had a small winder. He held the handset close to his ear and spun the winder. Dragon came on the line instantly. "Sir the enemy has opened heavy artillery fire on us, five rounds so far and highly accurate... with no cover we won't last long." Dragon said, "Yes Baaz I saw that, the enemy must have an OP (Observation Post) somewhere that is able to observe you and pass on information about all your movements and positions. I'll find and eliminate it, you hold steady."

Dragon turned his other phone's winder and said, "Get me Ice." Ice was at the other end in a second. Dragon spoke quickly, "Did you see the arty fire? It's accurate, they have an OP somewhere. Find him and finish him Ice and I mean as of ten minutes ago." Ice was already on the job. He had asked his fifty sniper teams to scan the area and find the OP. That wasn't easy because the OP would be as well-camouflaged as a sniper.

It was a sniper team from the Gorkha Battalion that responded four minutes later. They reported seeing a straight line high up on the ridge line. "How long is this straight line?" Ice asked. The Indian army teaches its soldiers early on in basic training that there are no straight lines in nature, straight lines are manmade. "At least three to four feet sir, it looks like an antenna." Sepoy Bahadur Singh of the Gorkha team replied. "Can you see any enemy personnel?" Ice asked. "No sir but I can see a tuft of grass which is thick enough to conceal a man." "Okay, use single shot but do not give away your position. Shoot to kill, immediately." Ice said in a flat toneless voice.

Sepoy Bahadur Singh was a Gorkha, one of the fiercest fighting soldiers the world has ever known. Gorkhas are known for their tracking, hunting and killing skills. The British Army had used them extensively in World War II and then again in the Falklands War against Argentina. Hunting came naturally to Bahadur. He hunkered down, adjusted his lens, aimed carefully and acquired his target. Then he stopped breathing and became completely motionless. Eight seconds later, he pulled the trigger of his trusted sniper rifle. The tuft of grass sprang to life, rocked and spewed a jet spray of dark liquid. Sepoy Dhansingh Negi, Bahadur's spotter and best friend commented, 'You've hit an artery.' The ground nearby suddenly ejected another tuft of grass that got up to run. Bahadur squeezed his trigger again and the second one fell motionless almost instantly. Bahadur continued to aim and fired a few more shots into the two now stationery tufts and then at anything that could be even vaguely suspicious. Moments later, the area was surely and certainly sanitized.

It was less than six minutes since Baaz had spoken to Dragon when his phone buzzed again and Ice said, "OP eliminated." Baaz put the handset back in its cradle. Those six minutes had been devastating; several more artillery shells had pounded his positions and caused crippling damage to his assault force.

Dragon leaned back and heaved a sigh of relief. "Thank God that's taken care of, that OP would have torn us to shreds." Wolf stayed silent. Ice seemed to be living up to his reputation, he led his men well in Phase one and efficiently snuffed out of the sniper. He would have got their respect by now but consistency in performance was vital.

Another phone rang; it was a direct line so Dragon knew whose call it was. He picked up the handset within a second. Brigadier Sher Ali Khan's voice boomed loud and clear. "Dragon, the enemy has escalated this conflict, his artillery has begun heavy barrages on our town ships. The civilian areas of Doonch district are being shelled heavily, more than fifty artillery shells have landed so far and the fire concentration is on Kalai Bridge. If that bridge is destroyed Dragon, we'll be forced to retaliate with heavier fire. That means a never-ending vicious cycle of escalation which could lead to a full- blown war between our two countries.

Eleven civilians were dead on last count, more could die as we speak and the bridge is in jeopardy. I've begun evacuation of civilians from the area, it's all you now, break their back. I want ruthless, merciless action. They've carved out a piece of India, our Motherland. Do you understand? Evict them with such force, speed and brutality that the shock will prevent them and their future generations from even thinking of entering here again."

Dragon managed to let a "Yes, Sir!" escape from his dry throat. He feared for the enemy if Brigadier Sher Ali Khan ever got down to the battlefield.

Green was a third generation army officer from Dehradun, soldiering was in his blood. Two generations before him had gloriously served in and eventually commanded the same unit of the Punjab regiment. He had joined the NDA (National Defense Academy) at the age of eighteen and then graduated as an officer from the IMA (Indian Military Academy) with the 'Sword of Honour'. He was commissioned directly into the Punjab Regiment.

Green was a pure vegan who stayed away from any animal products, including cheese, milk and eggs. Hence, the name Green. He had spent his childhood growing up in the same battalion so he knew every single soldier, their family backgrounds and their local issues. He identified with them and they loved him as they would a local crown prince. It was expected that in the tradition of the two generations before him, he too would become the Commanding Officer of this fine battalion one day.

Secure in his world, Green was a happy person who loved to laugh hard. Unlike Wolf and few others, Green never frowned at Ice; he in fact enjoyed his company because he had never encountered someone so different before. They were from two different worlds. They had become good friends and Ice had promised to take Green party-hopping in Bombay on their next leave... something new that Green was looking forward to.

Ram Singh reported to Baaz. Twelve of his men were dead, fourteen wounded. Manny's ears were bleeding and he was partially deaf but he refused to get evacuated and insisted on staying in the battlefield. Baaz looked at his watch: 2137h, less than two hours for the attack to start. He turned to Ram Singh who flinched as another enemy artillery shell landed close by. The enemy had not eased up on their shelling despite losing their OP. Though they still caused occasional damage, their fire wasn't as accurate now. Baaz needed to do something drastic to reenergize his assault team. "Find me a stick, same size as my official staff cane." Baaz said to Ram Singh who was confused but knew better than to ask. He scampered away on his haunches, keeping low to avoid enemy fire.

2300H 23RD AUGUST 1991

At 2322h, Baaz holstered his automatic pistol and strapped his Machine Carbine behind his back. Instead of these in his hand, all he held was his stick given by Ram Singh. He waved it around and charged forward up the hill toward towards the enemy, this was a tremendous motivation for his loyal soldiers.

As he led the assault, he shouted, "*Jo Bole Sonehal!*" Over a hundred Punjabis responded with a petrifying "*Sat Sri Akal!*" and charged ahead... it was a sight to see!

Jo Bole So Nihal, Sat Sri Akal or, 'Victory belongs to those, who recite the name of God with a true heart,' is an overpowering centuries-old battle cry that has motivated and empowered Sikhs to crush enemies across the globe including the Mughals, Afghans, Germans, Japanese, Sri Lankan Tamils, terrorists and other unfortunate ones who have stood at the receiving end of their assault.

The adversaries opened up with all that they had. The heavenly Pir Panjal ranges were ravaged with the staccato sounds of machine gun fire, missiles, mortars and other assorted instruments of death.

Several of Baaz's men were cut down but the assault continued undeterred. Stick in hand, Baaz ran up the hill with his loyal soldiers who ran side by side with him as they had done in the past. While running, Baaz turned to his sides to encourage his men. Next to him was Ram Singh who ran alongside firing accurately and ducking enemy fire at the same time. Suddenly an unexpected muffled explosion mushroomed from the ground; it catapulted Ram Singh and sent him spinning into the air and he landed in front of Baaz. Ram Singh was conscious and wide eyed; he stared back up at

Baaz and then looked down at himself in horror, his right leg had been severed below the knee, blood streamed out unabated.

'Mines! The enemy had used daylight to mine the area! But it was too late to do anything other than continue. Baaz continued to charge ahead. He could hear similar explosions on his left and right followed by screams of agony but his courageous soldiers charged on undeterred with him. The enemy fought back tooth and nail but to no avail. Indians were already amongst them inside their trenches and bunkers.

Manny, who had refused to get evacuated along with the other casualties, climbed up the hill behind the frontal wave. He still couldn't hear well but was improving by the minute and would be battle-worthy again soon. As he climbed forward, he came across Ram Singh who was still conscious and on his stomach. He was using his hands to drag what was left of his body toward cover in the ground that would protect him from enemy fire. He was pale from the loss of blood. Multiple waves of emotions rose within Manny. His heart beat so hard he thought he would pass out but instead he went straight for Ram Singh, turned him over on to his back and dragged him to safety holding his armpits.

Ram Singh was heavy and not easy to move; an enemy soldier saw Manny and Ram Singh as a slow, easy target and aimed at them. His first bullet hit the ground about three feet away from Manny. He adjusted his sights and fired again. The second round shattered a rock a few inches away from Ram

Singh. Manny knew it was a matter of seconds before he would be hit too but he didn't give up, he wasn't about to let Ram Singh bleed to death on the mountainside. Another shot rang out, it didn't hit Manny directly but went through his tunic and he felt it singe his stomach. The pain he felt was similar to that of being branded by a hot iron, he felt wetness spread around his battle fatigues along with the pain. He knew he was bleeding but he held on and continued to slip and struggle.

The enemy soldier corrected his aim, this time he had Manny clearly in his sights. He smiled in anticipation as he slowly increased pressure on his rifle trigger.

Just before he let loose his deathly round, an Indian soldier suddenly ran up and helped Manny pull Ram Singh into cover. They took refuge behind a few rocks and were safe for the moment, Ram Singh was now almost white, wheezing loudly and his eyes rolled around wildly. Manny looked around and yelled, "Medic!" It took several anxious moments before a medic turned up crawling to avoid being hit by enemy fire. The medic had a satchel slung around his shoulder. He placed it on the ground, tore it open and dug up a syringe. "Morphine," he said as he stabbed Ram Singh with it and then began tending to the injured man's stump.

Manny held Ram Singh's hand and sat by him till he lost consciousness. That's when he noticed that the soldier who had helped him drag Ram Singh to safety was Baaz's Sahayak Shaitan Singh. Manny distinctly remembered Baaz ordering

Shaitan Singh to stay back and not join the attack. He controlled the urge to order him back to base but he was himself there against orders and common sense so he chose to say nothing. He looked at Shaitan Singh and nodded an acknowledgement for helping save Ram Singh. Shaitan Singh nodded and ran to join the assaulting troops upfront.

At the front, Baaz had breached the enemy's lines, it was now cruel hand to hand combat that can be best described as barbaric. The enemy held on with every ounce of energy, strategy and sheer grit they had but Baaz and his men were beyond their league. A few of them surrendered, others panicked and ran upward towards their final rung of defense at the helmet-like top of Ring Contour. Those who chose to stay on and fight did so till their end. At 0534h on 23rd August 1991, Major Baaz picked up his handset and briefly spoke the words "tissue paper" into it. He then fell to his knees, exhausted.

Dragon who sat by his radio set in silence exhaled when he heard the words 'tissue paper.' It meant that the vanguard of the attack led by Baaz had succeeded but he controlled his elation because he hadn't heard the code words of success from Ice and Green yet.

On the left flank, as Ice darted up at the enemy positions, bullets whizzed past him, some so close that he could almost taste them but it didn't matter, he kept the pace and his men charged with him. The enemy was much better-prepared this time but that didn't matter because it didn't change a thing.

Ice would get what he had come for even if it meant dying for it. The enemy fought back malevolently but Ice and his team imposed victory on them swiftly.

At 0614h Dragon heard the word "Saaf" and knew that Ice had made it too. He waited breathlessly to hear Green say "Zip". Then he would know for sure that Phase 2 had been successfully completed.

On the right flank, Green charged, then took cover, fired and charged again. He moved tactically and his progress was steady. His NCO signalled towards a place in the mountain twenty meters away. It was an enemy bunker. Inside it were three enemy soldiers manning a well-covered medium machine gun. Green motioned to his NCO who in turn signalled to his troops behind. Within moments, two Indian soldiers crept forward with an 84mm rocket launcher, positioned themselves carefully and aimed at the enemy bunker.

A few seconds later, a ball of flame erupted as a back blast from the rear end of the rocket launcher and from the front end whizzed out an 84 mm projectile that went smack into the loophole of the bunker. There was a thunderous blast and dense smoke poured out. Green and his men waited thirty seconds before they charged into the bunker firing and killing anything that could possibly have survived the rocket attack. Once they made certain that it was completely sanitized, they moved quickly towards the next bunker.

All that remained for the completion of Phase 2 was one last bunker. It was flushed against a vertical face monitoring and punishing all movements below. Green's men let loose two rocket launcher rounds at it but they were unsuccessful because both exploded harmlessly against the rock face.

Green briefed his NCO who, along with four volunteers, took up position a little further away on the left. They then opened fire with an LMG (Light Machine Gun). Though it didn't destroy the bunker or kill the enemy, it annoyed and distracted them to an extent. Exploiting this distraction, Green and two of his trusted soldiers made their way quickly and stealthily upwards to the right of the bunker. Using all the expertise they had, they managed to sneak around it undetected.

Once behind the bunker, it took no time to locate the rear entrance. A narrow path about three feet wide slopped downward and led to a wooden door that was flushed to the ground. As Green and his men came closer, they could hear the enemy barking commands inside the bunker. Green motioned his two men to stay put and cover him as he whipped out two grenades and pulled the pins off both of them. The clips were still in place, held firmly in the palms of his hands. He approached the door cautiously and finally when he was close enough he readied his right leg to kick the door open and lob his grenades inside.

Without warning, a six-inch square window opened from the centre of the door and the barrel of a machine pistol sprung out. Green watched dumbstruck as it pointed straight at him and opened fire. He didn't stand a chance, his face contorted in disbelief, shock and pain as he watched himself get cut into two pieces that fell separately to the ground. As the two halves of Green hit the ground, his heartless grenades also rolled loose. Thanks to the slope, they both rolled to the bottom of the wooden door. Seven seconds later. there were two successive explosions, their combined impact ripped the bunker door apart and vapourized Green's corpse. His two soldiers lobbed at least six more grenades into the now doorless bunker...within moments it was all over. Phase 2 was a success but a very expensive one.

Dragon heard the word he had waited breathlessly for but he then also heard the detailed report. He sat motionless in his chair, a bundle of mixed emotions. He was delighted by the news of Phase 2 being a success but was equally devastated by the constant reports trickling in of casualties. Good men he had known for years were coming back either dead or injured. Some would be physically crippled for life; many would be permanently emotionally scarred. He would personally make calls to family members he knew so well and give them the terrible news. He would tell them that their husband/son/father/brother wouldn't be coming home alive.

7

0945H: 24TH AUGUST 1991

Major Green and several others were dead; many were severely wounded but Phase 2 was a success. Baaz had consolidated his position well enough to repel any counterattack. The enemy either realized that Baaz couldn't be dislodged easily or wasn't interested in even trying. They left most of their wounded behind to be taken prisoners, those who escaped retreated further upwards towards the top of Ring Contour.

Dragon and Baaz had a detailed discussion using their secure line. Baaz first gave an update on the situation at the front line. Dragon then gave Baaz a brief on the larger picture and how things looked from further behind including the heavy shelling of civilian areas like Doonch and Kalai Bridge. They discussed logistics; both agreed that Baaz urgently needed fresh well-rested soldiers for the final assault along with lots of ammunition, weapons, explosives, night vision devices, hot food, water, combat equipment, communication devices and medical support.

Baaz had already begun evacuating some of his wounded soldiers towards the rear. But he faced a dilemma which he discussed with Dragon. In such a mountainous terrain with no air support, all movement had to be on foot and was time consuming. Every wounded soldier needed two fighting fit soldiers to carry him out of the frontline. At the same time, every wounded soldier who lay writhing in agony affected the morale of his combat-worthy colleagues. Baaz needed to decide whether to denude his fighting strength to evacuate the immobile wounded or to make them wait next to the fit ones, affecting their morale till fresh troops arrived from the rear. Guarding the enemy prisoners further eroded Baaz's fighting numbers.

Both Baaz and Dragon agreed that their victories were well-earned but this enemy was definitely up to something. He definitely still had a few aces up his sleeve.

Perched high up above, the enemy fire covered approaches and this made movements to and fro from Ring Contour very challenging. The Indians had to use every rock, crack and opportunity for protection. However, there were patches of ground that afforded no cover whatsoever.

Both sides continued to assault each other with everything they had. They were equally determined to break the others' back. The enemy relied heavily on mortar and artillery fire to decimate or at least disrupt the Indian supply and logistics line known as 'axis of maintenance'.

Ice was about a hundred meters away from Baaz perched in a position from where he could see the enemy yet not be spotted by them. He directed sniper and artillery fire to provide cover for Indian troops trying to move in and out of the battle zone. The snipers had more or less lost their efficacy because the Indian team had captured over seventy percent of the monolithic Ring Contour which dwarfed all the surrounding hill features where the snipers had been positioned. Artillery, thankfully, was still of use but only for as long as there was a safe gap between the Indians and their enemy. Once the two adversaries were in close proximity to each other, it would be too dangerous to call for artillery support. Friendly fire was known to cause casualties in war.

Dragon and Baaz discussed the pros and cons of pursuing the attack and finishing off Phase 3 right away as against waiting till the next night. The enemy held the tactical advantage of weapons and position, while the Indians had success and an established axis of maintenance as their advantage. Time was running out because the enemy would sooner or later establish their own axis of maintenance that would give them a fresh consignment of weapons, soldiers and other supplies. Dragon and Baaz estimated that the enemy would need at least forty-eight hours to set up their axis. That was enough time for Baaz to get well-rested and battle-worthy troops to replace his fatigued soldiers on the frontline and then attack the next night. Even after that he would still have another twenty-four hours to consolidate his position and ensure that the enemy's counterattack plans were thwarted. It was almost 1100h, they needed to decide soon.

Brigadier Sher Ali Khan informed Dragon that all enemy shelling on Indian civilian areas had ceased a few minutes ago and they wondered why. At that very moment, a fresh batch of explosions ripped through a different side of the mountains. Ice stopped what he was doing and peeked out to understand this new event. Dragon and Baaz too put their call on hold to see what was happening.

The enemy had opened up concentrated heavy artillery fire on a vertical mountain face adjacent to Ring Contour. The strange thing was that there were absolutely no Indian troops there. It was in fact far off from where they were. "What are they doing?" Dragon asked Baaz who responded, "I have no idea sir."

Manny whose bleeding had stopped and hearing had improved too tried to make sense of the enemy action. The barrage hammered the same spot on the mountain face relentlessly and the Indians watched flummoxed. This continued for some time before Ice realized what was going on. The sheer brilliance of the enemy suddenly hit him like a sledgehammer. He leapt towards his radio set and Dragon was on the secure line in a few seconds. "Sir!" Ice said urgently, "They must have identified a weak spot on the cliff face, they are targeting a fault line in the hillside to trigger a landslide. If that happens, the collapsing vertical face will bury and bust our axis of maintenance. Sir, we must either stop them or create an alternative axis now!"

Dragon realized that Ice was right, he understood why the enemy had stopped shelling civilian areas; those guns were now trained at the weak spot on the mountain face. Dragon also realized that since the enemy heavy artillery guns were tucked away somewhere safe many kilometers away, there was very little he could do at this point to stop their brilliant scheme. He picked up another handset and yelled, "Wolf, they are firing at a soft spot in the vertical face to cause a landslide. Stop all fresh movement towards Ring Contour but push through those who are already under that zone. Also, double the speed at which we are pulling out our wounded from the battle zone and create another axis for me quickly. Wolf we have no time! Hurry!"

Lt Col Wolf looked out of his bunker through his binoculars. "Oh, No!" he said out loud.

Dragon got Baaz on the line. "Baaz, did you get all that?" "Yes, sir!" Baaz responded, he had heard both the conversations. "I've ordered the pushing through of our wounded first and then the enemy prisoners out of this battle zone sir. If there is a landslide and we get cut off, I will need every fighting man I have and won't be able to handle prisoners." Dragon agreed with Baaz and they both got down to doing what was needed to be done.

The inevitable began forty-seven minutes later with a rumbling sound that emanated from the heart of the mountain. Soldiers of both sides paused to see the sight, the rumbling evolved into a thunderous crash as an entire part of the mountain face peeled out and collapsed downward. Stones and debris snowballed and increased in size as they descended.

The cliff face continued to peel and collapse in layers. The base was covered with thick clouds of debris and dust. When it finally cleared many, many minutes later, the Indian axis of maintenance was completely destroyed. Dragon and Wolf watched from afar and thanked God they managed to clear their troops in time. Ice's quick understanding had saved many lives but with this one stroke, the enemy had turned the tide of battle in their favour. Now every trump card was with them. Ice watched from his perch, his mind was racing ahead to calculate forward. No supplies, no fresh rested troops, cut off completely. What next?

Manny and Baaz leaned out of their secure fold to watch the landslide. Baaz looked at Manny who reported, "All our wounded have crossed Sir, most of the prisoners too. We are safe on that score but ammunition, food, water and fresh troops are definitely a problem."

Baaz didn't move, his half-closed eyes remained as they were. Manny could tell that Baaz was in deep thought, he knew that look well enough but what happened next was too sudden and abrupt for him to even react. Baaz's forehead burst open with a spray of blood and he crashed backward from where he stood without even a moan. Manny moved right and then dived for cover. Once down, he looked across at Baaz whose face was now a mask of blood. He reached out and dragged Baaz's limp body into a sheltered area.

When he and Baaz had leaned out to watch the landslide, they had unknowingly exposed themselves and an alert enemy sniper had let off one round with his rifle. He knew he wouldn't get a second clear shot anytime soon so he had to make it count and count it did, Baaz was hit in the forehead.

Manny called the radio operator, "Get Ice here. He's in command now...hurry!" He then called for a medic and picked up the secure line. Dragon was already on the line, "Sir, Baaz is down sir, I repeat Maj Baaz is down."

Wolf bit his lip silently; the situation couldn't get any worse than this. Baaz, Green and Ram Singh had been written off, Manny's combat-worthiness was debatable; there were a handful of them on Ring Contour cut off from their supply lines with limited resources. They were up the creek without a paddle and Ice was the oarsman now. Did he have the mettle to handle such a situation? And even if he did, would the troops follow someone so new and so different? Wolf had his doubts about Ice's ability right from the beginning but now it was a question of time before the truth would be revealed. And he was in no hurry to find out.

8

1353H: 24TH AUGUST 1991

Ice took time to make his way to where Manny was when he finally did reach, he saw Baaz lying with his head bandaged securely. "Is he…" "Not yet Sir," Manny said, "The bullet grazed his forehead, he's lost a lot of blood; he's alive for now but won't last long, he's fading."

Manny briefed Ice and brought him up to speed on the latest developments, including logistics and the debate about the timing of their assault. Once he had got a grip on the situation, Ice spoke to Dragon on the secure line and discussed it for a few minutes. Creating a new axis of maintenance and sending fresh troops could take between sixteen and eighteen hours or maybe more depending on the weather and enemy fire. Finally Ice said, "Sir, we need to move now, I am launching Phase 3 with everything I have."

Alarmed and concerned, Dragon reacted, "How? Your troops are already exhausted and you don't have enough manpower."

Ice replied, "Sir we are cut off from you. This is the enemy's best chance to finish us off. If I don't attack now, he'll come down here to finish me off. If I don't act now, time will be on his side. My best form of defense here is offense sir."

"And where will you get enough fighting troops from?" Dragon asked.

"Sir we are going to have to power our way through this one. I'm going to take every fighting fit volunteer from Phases 1 and 2 with me and storm the enemy nest. If my attack fails, then our survivors, along with our semi-wounded and non-volunteers can fall back and still hold the two tiers of Phases 1 and 2. If I sit here and wait for him to come after me, we risk losing everything we worked for so far."

Dragon was silent for a moment. "You are right. As suicidal as it may sound, an attack is your best bet but bear in mind that this enemy is brilliant. He is retreating tactically to make you walk into his trap, don't underestimate him. Structure your plan on the premise that he is smarter than you. God bless you Ice, keep me posted."

Wolf stood with his arms crossed and his head down behind Dragon. He didn't utter a word but the expression on his face spoke for itself.

Ice turned to Manny, "Get all the battle-worthy boys here. I want to have a quick heart-to-heart talk with them. Hurry Manny, time is now on their side."

1530H: 24TH AUGUST 1991

Manny moved the wounded but rifle-worthy men downward

to Phases 1 and 2 to hold defenses. He then ordered every fighting fit man upward to the frontline where Ice was. Havildar (Sergeant) Rana Sodhi of First Platoon, Charlie Company, was in the first rung of Ring Contour when he received word that all fighting fit soldiers were to move up to the top. He had been among the first to rupture the enemy defenses in Phase 1. Since then the fighting had been severe and opportunity for rest nonexistent. Even when fresh food and equipment arrived from the rear, he had passed it on and sent it up top for the troops who were pushing the enemy further back up the mountain.

He was from Bakhlaur in Punjab and had fourteen years of service; he worshipped his unit officers Baaz and Green while Manny was his role model. When he heard of Green's death, he was distressed, later when the mountain face collapsed cutting them off, he thought they were in trouble but when he heard that Baaz was possibly dead, Rana Sodhi knew that they were desperate.

Rumour had it that Ice was now heading the entire operation. Rana anticipated the worst. He had come across Ice occasionally but had never interacted with him closely. They said he had a fine battle record but personally Ice seemed very different. He was well-mannered and respectful but he wasn't a typical officer, he dressed different, talked and walked different... he seemed to be from somewhere else. Rana asked himself if he was willing to trust someone so different with his own life and the lives of his men; his men trusted him so he owed it to them to be sure of what he was doing.

Rana had earned his stripes the hard way; life had taught him a lot and one of the bigger lessons was the difference between being brave and being courageous. Brave people were fearless, they jumped right in. Courageous people were aware of (the) risks and they felt fear, they were often gripped by it but they weighed their options judiciously before making decisions. If these decisions so demanded then they stood up to their fears, overcame them and went to do what needed to be done. Rana chose a long time ago to be courageous rather than brave.

Ice's leadership and actions in Phases 1 and 2 had proved that he was no coward but was he brave? Or was he courageous? During his fourteen years, Rana had come across a few young officers who were glory hunters, brave men. Their quest for splendor normally ended in death...their own and of the men who followed them. Would Ice lead them to victory or death?

Rana pondered over this issue; he needed to decide a future course of action for himself and his men. He looked at his fellow mates as they made their way to the top, only eighteen left of the original thirty six of First Platoon, Charlie Company. They were all tired, stressed out and had their apprehensions but there was a buzz amongst them, this is what the Khalsas lived for, they were in their element.

Rana decided that Ice's leadership had been stellar so far and if the Army had trusted him enough to make him an officer then he had earned the right to be heard. Rana would listen to him carefully and then decide which way to swing.

years of his service as a Sahayak taking care of Major Baaz and his family. He requested permission to join the assault and Major Baaz refused but he seems to have sneaked in anyway."

Ice knew that it was common for a soldier to skip live operations and action if he was a Sahayak and this one, Shaitan Singh, had spent all of his service as a Sahayak. His training and battle-worthiness were definitely questionable. What exposure to combat could he possibly have?

Ice spoke to Manny, "Get organized; we need six rotating waves for the assault, each team with ten claymore mines, flares and one automatic grenade launcher. Every section must have two Light Machine Guns and one Rocket Launcher. Every soldier must carry at least ten hand grenades, and not less than a thousand rounds of ammunition. Section leaders report to me for a briefing in fifteen minutes."

Manny was about to start executing Ice's orders when Ice held him back and said, "Send Lance Corporal Shaitan Singh to me right now."

Manny was off in a flash. His agility and speed never failed to impress Ice.

9

Hammering of heavy mortar shells, whining of rockets followed by the invariable boom and the anxiety of the oncoming attack looming large over their heads could have shaken any one's senses but it wasn't enough to keep Ice from marvelling at the breathtaking beauty of the Pir Panjal mountain ranges sprawled out in front of him. He understood the Mughal emperor Jehangir's fascination for them.

His chain of thought was broken by a tentative voice from behind him. "Lance Corporal Shaitan Singh reporting Sir."

Ice turned to face the wide-eyed, pockmarked soldier standing at complete attention.

Ice: "Lance Corporal Shaitan Singh, you have nine years of service is that right?"

Shaitan Singh: "Yes Sir."

Ice: "And all nine years have been as a Sahayak?"

Shaitan Singh: "Yes sir."

Ice: "Any live combat experience?"

Shaitan Singh: "No sir."

Ice: "When was the last time you fired an assault weapon?"

Shaitan Singh: "Maybe a year back sir."

Ice: "Why do you want to go on this op?"

Shaitan Singh: "Sir?"

Ice: "Why do you want to go on this op? Sit tight for a few more years and you can go home in one piece to your wife and kids. Then live off your pension and lead a charmed retired life. Why rock the boat after all these years?"

Shaitan Singh: "Sir, please don't reject my request. I need to be part of this operation."

Ice: "Why? Why do you want to volunteer for a high-risk mission like this? You know that what we are about to do is almost suicidal. We are as good as dead. Why not volunteer for normal patrolling and guard duties? Don't you want to grow old and play with your grandchildren?"

For the first time Shaitan Singh looked certain. He looked Ice straight in his eyes. Ice saw no fear or duress but he did see a measure of desperation in those innocent large eyes and he felt a warmth and affection for this soldier.

Shaitan Singh: "Sir, it's true that I have been a Sahayak for nine years. It's also true that I have not had much combat exposure but that's not why I came here. I didn't join the army to be a Sahayak. I was assigned as one and my dharma tells me to be the best I can be in any and everything I do. I did my best to be a good Sahayak. That's why I stayed as one for nine years. If I have to continue being one, I will still be the best I can be but that's my *dharma*, that's how my parents brought me up.

I joined the Army as a proud Sikh to serve my country... my Motherland. I polish shoes, boil milk and do everything else with all my heart because it's all a part of my duty and there is honour in every deed no matter how small but now nine years later, I've been labelled. In this company, they don't see Lance Corporal Shaitan Singh, they only see a Sahayak. Doing one does not make me incapable of doing the other. I am both, I am a Sahayak and a soldier as every Nihang is a Saint and a Warrior."

Shaitan Singh continued, "Since you don't know me personally, you are still free from prejudices and open enough to see me as a soldier. Please sir, give me this one opportunity to be what I waited to be all my life."

Ice: "But are you even combat-worthy? I doubt whether you are capable of handling a weapon or even the stress of battle."

Shaitan Singh: "Sir, I will not allow what I am to come in the way of what I want to be."

Ice was taken aback by the depth and power of Shaitan

Singh's statement but it was the conviction and passion in its delivery that impressed him the most.

Shaitan Singh continued, "Sir once I grow old and am unable to do things I now can, I will be filled with regret and longing. Please sir... you are my only hope. Please take me on this mission, I will not slow you down; I will not come in anyone's way. I have what it takes and am willing to do what it takes. I will be an asset to this mission. Please don't refuse."

Ice: "Where are you from?"

Shaitan Singh: "Moga district in Punjab Sir."

Ice turned to the inescapable beauty of the snowcapped mountains and remained quiet for a moment, he seemed to be inhaling and absorbing their power. Then he turned back and said, "Shaitan Singh from Moga district in Punjab, be careful what else you wish for today because your prayers are being answered. You will be in my detail, stay close to me Shaitan Singh... become my shadow. Get your gear and prepare yourself, there are horrors awaiting you out there tonight. May God bless you with all the courage and skill you need."

Shaitan Singh's pockmarked face broke into a wide grin, exposing crooked and uneven teeth. The joy in his face was explicit. He gave his best salute, "I am a Sikh sir, I was born ready. Jai Hind!" He said and he ran to join his mates.

10

1845H: 24TH AUGUST 1991

Ice and Manny took the section leaders stealthily to a vantage point from where they could view the fringes of the top of Ring Contour. They discussed the enemy gun nests and planned an assault route. It wouldn't be a straight one, they'd have to take several detours along the rock face to evade enemy fire and minimize casualties. The enemy, of course, knew they were coming and were waiting eagerly to rip them apart.

After working out the details they went back to their troops, loaded up and began their ascent up the cliff face. It was a steep, hard climb. On several occasions, they had to scale purely vertical patches and sometimes dangerous overhangs too. Breathless, hungry, exhausted, under heavy enemy fire but determined to a fault, they pressed on. No one seemed to be considering options even as a few soldiers fell victims to accurate enemy fire or simply slipped off into the ravines below.

Shaitan Singh was breathless and weary. His legs felt heavy as lead and shaky as jelly. He was terrified but he remembered Ice's instructions before they began their climb. Ice had wanted him to be his shadow. He used all his strength and kept close to Ice who was a few meters ahead of him; he observed Ice's climbing style and imitated him. He drew strength and composure from Ice who seemed so cool that he may as well have been snuggled up in bed, wrapped in a quilt and reading an engrossing novel.

He ignored his exhaustion but knew he wouldn't be able to go on much further; his body would eventually give up. He felt several emotions but quelled them all and tried his best to keep pace with Ice who was now quite ahead of him.

Almost like an answer to his prayers, he saw that Ice and the two scouts leading the advance had stopped. Ice gestured to the assault force and every single soldier became completely motionless. Shaitan Singh could almost hear the silence. He was exhausted; his legs felt like rubber. Suddenly a hand came up from behind him and wrapped itself around his mouth. Shaitan Singh jerked reflexively but the arm holding him was like unyielding steel, it even tasted like gunmetal…he couldn't even move his head. Slowly Manny emerged from behind him with a forefinger on his lips; Shaitan Singh understood that he was being told to stay silent. He didn't realize that he had been panting loudly out of sheer exhaustion. Once he was sure that Shaitan Singh would make no more sounds, Manny released his grip slowly then crawled soundlessly towards where Ice and the scouts lay silently.

Shaitan Singh knew something was afoot and followed Manny. As he neared Ice and the scouts, he could hear faint sounds but the sounds weren't being made by Ice or the scouts or even Manny…it was someone else!

Shaitan Singh hastened his pace, a vein on the side of his head pulsing with anticipation. As he came closer he could finally see what Ice and the rest were looking at; it was an enemy team and they were laying mines. There were at least nine of them working silently but feverishly, one of them was standing tall and overseeing the hasty operation; the rest were on the ground on all fours laying and concealing mines. Shaitan Singh figured that the one standing must be the one in charge, probably an officer. He was about six feet tall and unlike the others he wore a jap-cap instead of a helmet. He was fair and extremely handsome. He watched over his men and occasionally scanned the area around him with quick economical movements... he showed no signs of pressure.

Shaitan Singh was captivated, he couldn't peel his eyes off the man and he continued to stare open-mouthed as the man went about his business with calculated precision. Shaitan Singh would have continued staring completely fascinated the way a normal person would stare at a film star or a high ranking politician but the young man paused as if he sensed something, he turned as if in slow motion toward the hidden Indians and locked his eyes directly with Shaitan Singh.

Shaitan Singh froze...he knew he had been spotted. He wanted to become invisible but couldn't move a muscle. The young man was as fast as lightning. Without taking his eyes off Shaitan Singh, he moved smoothly, brought out his automatic pistol and pointed it straight at his target...his intent was clear but Shaitan Singh remained paralyzed despite knowing that death was imminent.

There was a burst of gunfire and Shaitan Singh flinched expecting to get hit and die but instead it was the young man and three of his colleagues who fell to the ground like nine pins. Shaitan Singh realized that Ice, Manny and the two scouts had already picked their targets and fired when they realized that Shaitan Singh had been spotted. The rest of the enemy soldiers scrambled for their weapons, two of them were already lying down flat inside a groove in the ground manning a deadly light machine gun which sprang to life spewing fire and death.

An Indian soldier grabbed Shaitan Singh by his belt and jerked him backwards bringing him harshly to the ground just in time as the light machine gun swept across where he had been a second ago. "You idiot, you'll get us all killed!" someone growled at him but Shaitan Singh kept his eyes on what was happening in front. Ice didn't seem even slightly fazed by the light machine gun. He gestured at his two scouts, who dug into their packs and pulled out a grenade each. On Ice's count "Seven, Six, Five, Four, throw!" all three of them tossed their grenades behind the fold where the enemy lay. Two seconds later there were three muted explosions and Shaitan Singh watched spellbound as body parts of the enemy soldiers and their light machine gun flew fifteen feet into the air along with a shower of blood, stone and debris.

Manny sprang out of his cover with a spine-chilling Punjabi war cry "Jo *bole sone haal…*" and charged ahead. The Indian assault team leapt to its feet, instantly shouting "*Satsri akal*" and charged with him. The shocked and confused enemy tried to realign themselves and put up a fight but they stood no chance, the Indians cut through them like a hot knife through butter... no prisoners were taken.

Shaitan Singh too had charged with his fellow soldiers but no war cry had escaped his lips. His throat was parched and his hands shook. He didn't fire a single round, in fact, he ran slowly as others passed him by. When the attack was over and the area had been sanitized, Shaitan Singh slumped into a crumpled heap on the ground; he retched and vomited several times over, his arms shook uncontrollably. A few other soldiers patted him on his back and calmed him till Manny arrived. Manny reached down with one hand, held Shaitan Singh by his collar and pulled him up onto his feet.

Shaitan Singh could feel Manny's breath on his cheeks; he focused at Manny's blackened face which was caked with mud, dried blood and sweat. His beard was matted and stuck to his face. "Stand up soldier," Manny growled. "You are going through an adrenaline rush, it will pass by. You almost got us all killed back there with your stupidity. We are in the midst of combat...you pull yourself together young man, any moves endangering the rest of us and I will shoot you myself. Is that clear? Have you understood me?"

Terrified, Shaitan Singh gathered his wits together and managed to mumble a "Yes, Sir!"

"Now drink a few sips of water and start acting like a soldier," Manny said as he let go of him. Shaitan Singh quickly pulled out his water bottle and took in a few large gulps of water. His hands still shook uncontrollably, spilling half the water onto his face.

A little calmer now, Shaitan Singh began to understand what had happened back there. Ice and the two scouts had already marked their targets, they were simply watching to understand the pattern in which the mines were being laid so that they could cross the minefield without anyone getting hurt. He felt terrible; he had behaved like an imbecile and almost got everyone else killed. If anyone had died there, Shaitan Singh was sure it would have been his fault. If only he had remained still and allowed Ice to figure out the entire pattern. Major Baaz was right. This was no place for him, maybe a good Sahayak is all he would ever be, nothing more... ever.

A few minutes later, they began their ascent again. Shaitan Singh wanted to lead the way out of sheer guilt but it was Ice and his two scouts who stayed upfront. What may have been thirty minutes seemed like a lifetime to Shaitan Singh. They moved in a single file with each soldier following the exact footsteps of his predecessor. They maintained a gap of at least ten meters between each other so that if a mine did go off, it wouldn't kill more than one soldier. They were led by Rana Sodhi, who used his bayonet to plough the ground before inching forward. With each step he took, Shaitan Singh thought his heart would explode. Rana Sodhi was an expert, he steered them brilliantly through the entire minefield without any mishaps. Once across, Ice stood taking a head count, he patted every soldier on the shoulder as they went past him in a single file.

Shaitan Singh could feel his cheeks burn with embarrassment. He kept looking down so that he could avoid making eye contact but as he reached, he felt Ice's hand on his shoulder. He looked up, ready to burst into tears of shame but Ice spoke comfortingly, "Any chain is only as strong as its weakest link and you my friend are not going to be that weakest link. Not now, not today and not ever. I have tremendous faith in you, more than you have in yourself and the team needs you. We all make mistakes, please don't repeat them."

Shaitan Singh sputtered, "Yes Sir! It won't happen again Sir. I swear to you." Ice gently patted his back and let go of Shaitan Singh who vowed in his heart that he would never let Ice down again.

The Indian team advanced steadily despite the fatigue and exhaustion that attacked them along with the enemy's fire, their steely resolve unshakable.

They finally stopped when Manny made a hand gesture, everyone stayed still except the section leaders who moved up to join him. They reached the fringes of the helmet like top of Ring Contour…their assault line. Shaitan Singh willed his arms and legs to rest and recover quickly. He understood that the final assault was only moments away. Ice surveyed the patch in front of them; there was now no cover left.

Since they had decided to maintain complete radio silence till the final attack actually started, there was no way for Wolf or Dragon to know what was going on. Back in the Ops

Room, Dragon was beside himself with anxiety. His thoughts were running amok. 'Will they make it? Will I lose more of my family tonight? My boys are out there and here I am helpless, there's nothing I can do about it but sit and wait.' He remembered his combat-worthy days and wished he was fifteen years younger; he would be leading the assault in place of Ice. Frustrated, he slammed the palm of his hand down on his desk.

11

2231H: 24TH AUGUST 1991

The journey up to this point had been a very expensive one. Several men had died and many were wounded but Ice knew that this last fifty meter stretch could be the worst. They had climbed up to this point using the slope and shrubs as cover but now the ground had levelled out. They were exposed from now on.

Ice turned and looked at his men; hardnosed warriors of the Punjab Regiment... the mighty Punjabis – pride of the Indian Army. Within the last few hours, they had climbed hills, faced bullets, killed fellow humans and watched their best friends fall in battle. The physical and emotional drain had been very heavy but they were highly motivated and trained soldiers who were willing to give whatever it took to get the job done. They weren't ordinary men anymore; they were giants who had the courage to stand for what they believed in regardless of the consequences. Bursting with anticipation yet disciplined, they awaited his signal to unleash their fury on the waiting enemy.

Ice knew that in a frontal assault of this kind, it's all or nothing. Once past the assault line and out in the open, there would be no stopping halfway, it was either kill or get killed.

He quickly checked what he had. His assault rifle was fully loaded, bayonet fixed, magazines loaded, grenades in place, automatic pistol loaded and holstered. Harnesses, laces, complete equipment all tied right... no loose ends. One can't afford to have an undone shoelace during an assault. His soldiers quickly did the same.

This was it... the moment of truth.

Dragon sat silently. Wolf had worked hard to set up a new axis of maintenance. Dragon's mind was completely with Ice and his men.

Back home in Bombay, Ice's friends were busy on their phones fixing their dates and tying up their party plans for the evening. After all, they had worked hard all day and had earned their fix of fun.

Back in the battle zone on Ring Contour there was no looking back. Ice finally gave the signal. The blood-curdling Sikh war cry shattered the night, "*Jo bole sone haaaal*" A chorus rang out as his soldiers responded, "*Sat Sri Akal*".

In an instant, both sides opened up with everything they had. Smokescreen shells, flamethrowers, machine gunfire, rockets, multicoloured flares, tracers, grenade blasts and mortar shells exploded as the Punjabis ran out into the open stretch for their direct frontal assault.

They ran side by side next to each other as only brothers in arms could... closer than blood brothers could ever hope to be.

As they reached halfway through the open patch, a deafening new sound broke loose. It dwarfed all the other sounds of the night; it was a heavy machine gun. But this was no ordinary gun, it was a .50 caliber heavy machine gun, the kind fitted on battle tanks to fire at aircraft and armoured vehicles. It spat out armour-piercing cannon shells at the rate of three to five hundred rounds per minute! Anything in its path was simply decimated. It was placed on the rightmost corner of the hilltop; its enfilade fire cut through the Indian assault. It had been kept silent and undiscovered all along; it was the enemy's final trump card.

Colonel Dragon's words rang out in Ice's mind. "This enemy is brilliant."

Ice watched in horrific slow motion as his foremost soldier, Sepoy Dalbir Singh, suddenly became headless. His lifeless body crumbled to the ground. Next was another soldier whom Ice could not recognize since he had been cut into three unidentifiable pieces in less than a second. Then right in front of Ice, Balwinder Singh turned to pulp from above his waist. Ice felt warm blood, shattered bones and flesh splash on him.

He already knew he was next in the line of fire but got no reaction time. He was slammed in the chest and flung off his feet. He flew backwards, his legs rose to the sky as he hit the ground flat on his back unable to breathe or move; he couldn't breathe and his right arm didn't seem to respond. He reached out for his chest with his left... it felt warm and wet. He then brought his hand in front of his face and saw his fingers covered with blood. The noises of combat were getting softer and all he could hear now was the wild thumping of the heavy machine gun or was it his heart?

The night sky was alive with colours, white tracer rounds dotted the sky, plumes of yellow, orange, blue, green and red flames mushroomed around him. Flares of multiple hues lit up the night, snowflake crystals, blood, bones, flesh and dust flew around freely. The once clear mountain air was heavy with the smell of gunpowder, burnt flesh, fear and death.

Ice felt himself slip into the abyss of death; the only thought in his mind was, 'My final assault has stopped halfway. This should never have happened....'

From an idyllic childhood in Bombay to a battlefield on an obscure mountain top on the Line of Control, it had been quite a journey but what life is worth living if you have nothing worth dying for?

Blackness tightened its noose, engulfing Ice. Yet, he knew that there was no other place on earth he would rather be... all sounds and lights faded and he felt himself slipping away into a void.

Silence... blackness... stillness... nothing.

12

Shaitan Singh worked his body the best he could to keep pace with Ice but his lack of mountain skills and stamina made it very difficult. He began to lose confidence as he watched others overtake him effortlessly in their maddening head-on charge at the enemy.

Ice was far ahead when the Heavy Machine Gun thundered out of nowhere, obliterating everything in its line of fire. Shaitan Singh's horror knew no bounds when he saw the evil gun's bullets hit Ice twice within a fraction of a second. First there was an eruption of blood from his right arm and at the same time, he was hit again square in the chest. Ice flew backwards and landed on the ground.

The rest of the assault team dove down hugging mother earth to avoid being killed by the murderous gun.

A panic attack seized Shaitan Singh. Without Ice to look up to and follow, he was like a headless chicken. 'What am I doing here?' he thought to himself. Fear crept around, inside and all over him like ants on a mound of sugar. He wanted to get up and run back downhill but was forced to lie flat on the ground as the bloodthirsty heavy machine guns bullets hit the ground so close to him that dust and dirt flew into his open mouth. He tried to turn his head to look for an escape route but that miniscule movement was enough for a bullet to ricochet off his helmet. It wasn't a direct hit, so his helmet protected him but his head still felt like a golf ball that had been hit with a full swing of a club. He froze and pressed his face further down, sure that he was going to die. His limbs shook uncontrollably and he began to cry.

Tears of anguish rolled out of his eyes and onto his dirt-stained cheeks. Then, they fell down on his Motherland where the soil sucked them in and they disappeared as if she were wiping them off.

Shaitan Singh shut his eyes tight and stayed still. Slowly, his shaking reduced as he felt himself being enveloped by an inexplicable calm. Then, in a surreal manner, he heard his grandfather's voice clearly as if he were standing six inches away. His doting grandfather was a deeply pious man who had read out to Shaitan Singh from the Guru Granth Sahib Ji for years during his childhood. It was almost a decade since he had passed away and Shaitan Singh missed him sorely.

He distinctly heard his grandfather recite the Sikh *Mool Mantar* exactly as he had countless times before. The *Mool Mantar* begins the *Guru Granth Sahib Ji* and defines the basic belief of the Sikhs.

'*Ek Onkar Sat Naam Karta Purakh Nir Bhau Nir Vair Akaal Moorat Ajooni Saibhang Gur Parsaad*'

"What does that mean?" Kim asked.

Indu responded, "It has several implications but here's a simplified translation for you:

Ek Onkar:	There is only One God
Sat Naam:	Truth is his name
Karta Purakh:	He is the creator
Nir Bhau:	He is without fear
Nir Vair:	He is without hate
Akaal Moorat:	He is immortal, without form
Ajooni:	He is beyond birth and death
Saibhang:	He is self-illuminated
Gur Parsaad:	He is realized by the kindness of the true Guru.

Shaitan Singh opened his eyes slightly now and saw that the mayhem was still on. The situation hadn't changed at all. They were still pinned to the ground but what had changed was his grandfather's tone as he now recited the Sikh anthem written by Guru Gobind Singh Ji.

'*Deh Shiva bar mohe ihai shubh karman the kabhu na taroo, Na daroo ar siyoo jab jah laroon. Nischai kar apni jeet karoo. Ar Sikh hao apne hi mun ko eh lalch hou guna tau uchroo jab aav ki audh nidhann banay aut he rann me tab joojh maroo.*'

And before you ask, here is the translation.

Deh Shiva bar mohe ihai:	Grant me this boon O God

Shubh karman the kabhu na taro:	May I never refrain from the righteous acts
Na daroo ar siyoo jab jah laroon:	May I fight without fear all foes in life's battles
Nischai kar apni jeet karoo:	With confident courage claiming the victory
Ar Sikh hao apne hi mum ko:	May thy glory be grained in my mind
Eh lalch hou guna tau uchroo:	and my highest ambition singing thy praises
Jab aav ki audh nidhann nanay:	When this mortal life comes to end
Aut he rann me tab joojh maroo:	May I die fighting with limitless courage

Now there was palpable change, it originated from within but slowly worked its way outward. Shaitan Singh's fear was chased away by courage and determination, his eyes focused. A new power surged through his being; he knew the risks involved but he knew that this was what he had been born for. His entire life was merely preparation toward this defining moment… it was now or never.

He gripped his rifle tightly and prepared himself.

13

As if breaking the surface after being submerged underwater for a long time, Ice burst back into consciousness gasping for air. He tried to get up but realized that his own men had held him down.

Manny said, "Sir a bullet that killed Balwinder Singh went through him and hit you in the chest right on your spare magazines. You are really lucky because Balwinder, his packs and equipment, your equipment and your magazines put together stopped it before it went through you."

Ice quickly gathered himself. They had covered half of that exposed last stretch when the enemy had opened up a surprise heavy machine gun. Three of his men had died before he was hit. He looked at his hands and felt his chest again…it was still blood-soaked. Manny spoke again, "Balwinder's blood sir."

That made sense but the right arm of his tunic was cut off right from the shoulder, leaving his arm exposed. The same rag was now tied around his bicep area. He felt both a stinging pain and a dull throbbing ache on the outside of his arm four inches from his shoulder.

Manny explained, "Another round ripped the skin and flesh

of your arm but there is no damage to your bone. Harbhajjan here sowed it together and I put a plaster on it to stop the bleeding."

By now Ice was completely reoriented, he looked at his arm, "Right on my Kavvach tattoo... it will be an ugly scar that will make for a great story over dinner some day but first let's complete this mission and make it out of here alive, we are in quite a pickle." Ice got up with a smile and a wink.

He took stock of the situation. His arm was a mess but it still worked, his chest hurt, he couldn't breathe or speak easily... maybe a couple of broken ribs were causing all the problems. He would have to shelve all the pain and deal with it much later; no time for that now because there were far more important issues at hand. His attack had come to a grinding halt... helplessly pinned down, urgent and decisive action needed to be taken or they would all be dead very soon.

Manny spoke again, "Three man .50 caliber heavy machine gun inside a very well fortified bunker cutting across our line with enfilade fire. We managed to drag you to safety but we lost Rana Sodhi, Balwinder, Harmeet and Dalbir."

There were few options in such situations.

First: Bring up a rocket launcher and blast the bunker.

Second: Provide exact coordinates to the mortar and artillery boys who would trash the bunker immediately.

Third: Go there physically and throw a grenade into the bunker the enemy was firing from.

"RL" (Rocket Launcher), Ice croaked to Manny who looked back and said, "Did that while you were unconscious sir, it's of no use. We were unable to get a direct hit, they are really well entrenched."

The enemy was really close, calling in artillery or mortar support would mean that his own team could get butchered by 'friendly fire'. Dismay began to creep in. They were unable to move, someone would have to silence that heavy machine gun before all of them got killed.

Manny heard it first. Then, Ice heard it too… it was a crazy, insane scream that emanated from behind them. Ice realized that it was one of his own men. Even before he could turn his head to look, someone ran past him.

The Indians watched in amazement as one of their own got up against all reasoning, kept screaming the Punjabi battle cry with his assault rifle in both hands above his head and ran head on towards the enemy.

The heavy machine gun roared angrily but this soldier charged on regardless. In fact, he ran directly towards the gunfire. Call it divine intervention or luck or destiny but not a single bullet touched him… within moments, he reached and was at the bunker.

It was a well-constructed bunker, melded into the ground.

Its walls were at least four feet thick with rectangular window-like slits about three feet wide and one foot high for the soldiers inside to see and fire through at the oncoming enemy. In local military language, these slits were called loopholes.

Manny, Ice and their remaining band of volunteers watched as their only hope miraculously reached the bunker but they couldn't make sense of what he did next. Once there, he aimed his assault rifle at the walls of the bunker and pumped bullets as if he expected it to give way. Within seconds, he emptied the entire magazine and his bullets were over. What he did next startled them even more… he held his rifle with both hands by the barrel and swung it over his head at the bunker wall like a lumberjack would chop wood with an axe!

Nothing happened so he kept hitting the wall with all his might. By the fifth swing, his rifle butt broke off and the weapon was rendered useless. He stood confused right next to the loophole from within which the heavy machine gun reverberated keeping the Indians constricted with their heads down.

He turned to look at his mates for their inputs. One managed to shout out over the din of battle, "Throw a grenade into the loophole." He understood instantly and pulled out a grenade from his front chest pouch. He then quickly lobbed it into the loophole.

Their grenades had seven-second fuses. All the Indians counted seven seconds in their minds as the grenade slipped into the loophole…

One...
Two...
Three...
The enemy had made a channel at the base of the loophole inside the bunker. The grenade went in, rolled out and finally spun to a lazy halt at the Indian soldier's feet. He stared at it in hapless disbelief.

As Dragon had warned "This enemy is very brilliant".

Four...
Five...

A heavy cloud of gloom settled on the Indian soldiers. They were unable to move and their one hope that had made it to the enemy bunker would die in a few seconds...

Six...
Seven...
Seven...
Seven...?
Seven???

An Indian soldier yelled, "You have to remove the pin before you throw the grenade you idiot!!" A wave of nervous yet relieved laughter rang through Ice's team but it didn't provide any solutions to the situation.

"Who is that?" Ice asked Manny who quickly responded, "Don't know sir, can't identify him."

Then, the Indian soldier at the bunker did something that no military manual anywhere in the world would have recommended. He reached into the loophole and grabbed the barrel of the heavy machine gun as it emotionlessly thudded on dispensing death and destruction. He screamed in agony but refused to let go, he pulled and pushed the barrel violently till its supporting tripod within the bunker lost balance and folded. Inside the bunker, three enemy soldiers wrestled to get it back on its stand. They succeeded in a few seconds but for that brief time, the fire lifted from the Indians.

This window of opportunity was all that Ice and his team required to slip through past its deadly line of fire. They leapt to their feet and charged with every ounce of Qi, the Chinese for life energy they had in them with their guns blazing with every step they took. The violent sounds of gunfire, grenade, mortar, rocket and other assorted instruments of death were drowned by the petrifying Punjabi war cry *"Jo bole sone haal!"*

Like a pack of determined and hungry Lions pouncing on a herd of Antelope, Ice and his team were upon the enemy defenses, kicking up a storm. Unable to stay constricted inside his bunker, a young enemy officer charged out straight towards Ice, spraying bullets as he ran. Ice saw his adversary, aimed and squeezed his trigger to return fire but nothing happened. He realized that his rifle magazine was empty; he was out of bullets! There was no time to reload. So he didn't slow down or pause… he simply weaved and zigzagged narrowly, escaping each bullet intended for him and ran into the attacking officer with full body force. Their bodies bumped directly into one another, their faces three inches apart. Ice's ten-inch rifle bayonet sliced through the man's rib cage and its sharp pointed tip came out of the other end.

The mortified enemy officer's life force dimmed, his legs gave away as he slumped forward. His mouth opened and a steady stream of blood and body fluids poured out onto Ice's shoulder who quickly snapped on a fully loaded magazine into his rifle and cocked it as a second enemy officer charged forward firing at him. The now very dead enemy officer's body took the bullets for him and Ice went down to the ground backward under the dead body as it leaned forward and fell on him.

The second officer now charging him was a young Captain. His eyes were ablaze with a mix of hate, fear and violence. He thought Ice was helpless under his dead colleague but three feet short of his mark he felt as if someone had punched him in the stomach. The wind was knocked out of him... he felt no pain, just a massive whack. A second later he felt another similar hit on his right arm. He turned to look and saw his entire arm already on the ground still holding his pistol. He felt himself drop to his knees and stayed there kneeling upright looking as Ice got up from under his dead friend. His mind wrestled with the sequence of events to make sense of what was going on. He concluded that Ice had shot him from under and through the body of his dead colleague.

He motionlessly watched as Ice moved like a jungle cat, never taking his eyes off him. Slowly he felt his body keel backwards from his kneeling position and he fell on his back with his feet tucked under him. All he could see now was the vast expanse of the sky. Not as many stars as any other night because tonight the air was almost opaque. He tried to turn his head to see where his severed arm lay but he couldn't move. Unmindful of the battle that raged on, blissfully carefree winds kissed his face and lovingly played with his hair, his mouth seemed to be filling with liquid... probably blood and bile.

He could hear himself gurgle and cough as he choked. He saw Ice standing next to him, looking somewhere else. Now he couldn't hear anything anymore, even his pain was overcome by numbness. He thought of his parents and was saddened that he would never get to say good bye properly to them, he wanted them to know how much he loved them. No sounds now, in the silence he saw Ice's rifle muzzle flashing in the direction of his men. Ice began to stride away but before that, without a pause or looking, his rifle pointed directly at the valourous Captain's forehead; he died a soldier's death. Ice moved on without batting an eyelid.

A common physics question asked in classrooms is, 'What happens when an unstoppable force meets an immovable object?'

This was as close as one could get to an answer. The attackers and the defenders were well beyond the point of no return. The occupying soldiers had nowhere to retreat to... this was their final stand. They dug in and fought hard and the Indians, outnumbered, low on equipment, food, water and energy, wouldn't relent until they got back every inch of their Motherland. What followed was a night of violent and bloody battle; it was savage violence at its worst. Brutal hand to hand combat with bayonets, rifle butts and bullets fired at point blank range. No quarter was asked and no quarter was given.

In this case, it was finally the unstoppable force that won.

0547H: 25TH AUGUST 1991

By the break of dawn the operation was as good as over. The entire Indian territory had been recaptured. The remaining few enemy soldiers were being hunted down.

When all of Ring Contour was finally sanitized and secured, Ice stood atop the highest point on its peak with Manny next to him and hoisted an Indian flag. As it fluttered, brandishing its beautiful colours, every Indian soldier, wounded or otherwise, saluted and cheered loudly amidst shouts of *Jai Hind*. Pent up emotions were finally unleashed, some collapsed, some laughed and some cried uncontrollably.

Manny was a pillar of strength. He didn't shake or cry or laugh, he simply reached down and picked some gravel with his fingers, wiped it across his forehead and mumbled audibly to himself, "*Maa, twada munda tere lai tere kol agaya.*" 'Mother your son has come for you.'

Back in Dragon's Ops Room, the atmosphere was euphoric; there was a lot of cheer and backslapping. After taking Dragon's permission, a hugely relieved Wolf left to continue overseeing the work that was feverishly on to create a new axis of maintenance. It would be up soon and after that no enemy counterattack could dislodge the Indians again. There was still work to do but the worst was over. Dragon ordered the rest of his team to leave the Ops Room and take a ten-minute break. Once alone, he looked around to ensure that no one was watching and then danced the jig merrily. Few knew that when he grinned unabashedly, he looked like a twelve-year-old boy.

Daylight arrived, chasing away the darkness. Ice had been right about the weather. Snowflakes began to drift downward from the sky as the sun shone through and a beautiful rainbow appeared shimmering like a message from the heavens that order had been restored from chaos. There was jubilation all around.

Ice was his trademark self, his face conceded neither the pain of his injuries nor the elation of a well-earned victory. He simply went about checking their defenses and preparing for a possible counterattack from the enemy. As he walked around, he eventually came toward the bunker where the heavy machine gun had been. He remembered how close they had come to being completely annihilated there. Nearer, he identified the shape of a soldier at the loophole of the bunker. It was one of his men. Hearing Ice's footsteps, the soldier raised his head and for the first time, thanks to daylight, Ice recognized him instantly… "Shaitan Singh!!"

It was Shaitan Singh who had charged the bunker like a mad man and it was Shaitan Singh that who had saved them all from certain death and defeat. Ice was overjoyed. After all it was he who had decided to take Shaitan Singh along on the assault against all logic. Ice stepped up his pace as he walked towards him.

"Shaitan Singh," Ice shouted. "Yes sir," Shaitan Singh responded. "I am proud of you my boy, you saved us all… you sprang forward and took the lead after all of us had stopped."

Shaitan Singh said, "Thank you, sir!"
Ice had to speak with gaps because of the pain in his chest. He was sure he had fractured at least two ribs. You will get full credit for this," he said.

Shaitan Singh responded, "Thank you, sir!"

Ice continued, "I will make sure you get the highest Medal of Honour, a Param Vir Chakra for this."

Shaitan Singh replied, "Thank you, sir!"

As he came nearer, Ice realized that something was not right.

Ice said, "Shaitan Singh, thanks to you the battle is over and we have won. You can get up now."

Shaitan Singh whispered, "I wish I could sir."

It was then that Ice saw what had actually happened.

In that moment of maddening commitment and passion,

Shaitan Singh had fearlessly grabbed the barrel of the heavy machine gun and dislodged it from its tripod. By then it had already been firing for quite a while and the barrel was red hot. So hot in fact that it burnt through his skin, seared through his flesh and when it finally cooled down as the firing stopped, the cold unyielding metal had welded itself against the bones of his palms and fingers. It was so deeply embedded that the barrel of the heavy machine gun had to be dismantled and cut. Shaitan Singh had no choice but to hold on to it while he was sent to base hospital where it was finally surgically detached from him.

That was August 1991.

Shaitan Singh eventually recovered from his injuries and even got a 'Kirti Chakra' for his heroism. He did not retire in 1994, instead he went on to serve for several years during which he participated in and led many other operations. Stories of his deeds over the years reached mythical proportions. The legend of Shaitan Singh often reached his enemies before he did. Some believed that Shaitan Singh transformed into a thirty-foot giant with vampire fangs and sucked his enemy's blood and would become normal only after he had eaten every beating heart alive. Such absurd exaggerations only helped him as the enemy often panicked and fled before he could get there. In one hostage situation, the hostage taker was simply told that Shaitan Singh was on his way. That was enough for him to surrender without a fight!

He was awarded for his bravery several times over. He became a Sergeant, then Sergeant Major. He didn't stop there; he went on to become a Lieutenant, then a Captain. He finally retired from service hale and hearty as an honorary Major and the most decorated soldier of his entire regiment. As an officer with such a fine combat record, he had earned a battle nickname for himself but it didn't stick because nothing came close to his own name so he was simply known as 'Shaitan - the Devil'. He now lives with his large brood of children in Moga district of Punjab as a living legend, an inspiration for many. His story provides hope where some of us have none."

"What about the others? I mean Manny, Ice, Sher Ali Khan, Baaz and the rest?" Brijesh asked.

Indu replied, "Let's start with Sher Ali Khan. He was a visionary who was recognized and duly awarded. He rose to the rank of Vice Chief of Army Staff. He was a man on a mission, his singular aim was to completely wipe out any kind of religious, geographical, caste or gender-based identification within the Army. He wanted officers to earn their respect by the merit of their performance, not by caste or creed.

He called his concept project 'Anamika' meaning 'anonymous'. It was to be executed over a span of fifteen years by the end of which all distinctions would be phased out of the officer grade and the army would be one unified, seamless unit protecting one unified nation. Sher Ali Khan had nothing against any religion or caste. He was in fact a pious man who did his namaz at least five times every day but he believed that labels make us jump to conclusions and make assumptions about people. As long as communal identification existed, we would be unable to understand any one's true potential. Sadly, Lieutenant General Sher Ali Khan died in a tragic helicopter crash somewhere in Meghalaya."

"What happened to Project Anamika?" Sandy asked.

"Some say it died with him while others whisper that his dream lives on and Anamika has been set into motion and that Indian Army officers will someday be free of caste and communal distinctions.

Dragon retired and took up a job as the head of security of an IT firm in Ahmedbad. He lives there with his wife and two daughters.

Baaz, Ice, Ram Singh, Manny and Shaitan Singh are still in touch. They are the best of friends even today. Baaz has taken over his father's vast lands and is a benevolent landlord who takes great care of his farmers. Baaz also financed Ram Singh who now runs his own manufacturing unit which specializes in prosthetic limbs. His products are fabulous but not being a very savvy businessman he doesn't make much money. Most of the time, he winds up donating his prosthetic limbs to soldiers wounded in combat."

"What about Manny?" Sandy asked.

"Manny runs one of the most successful security agencies in the country. Using his company's services is almost like a status symbol today.

"Which one?" Sandy asked but Kim stopped him short and asked, "And Ice? What about him?"

"That wasn't Ice's first or last combat mission; he was back in Kavvach and headed many operations till he was grievously injured in a blast. He spent almost two years in various hospitals where Army doctors eventually patched him up. He moved on to become a businessman; he's around and manages to break even."

"Ice is my role model, cool as a cucumber... what a man!" Kim said

Ishra shot back, "Manny any day, he's a pillar. Unmoving and solid like a rock."

"General Sher Ali Khan gets my vote. Visionaries are way ahead of the rest," Sandy said and Nadia thumped her desk in agreement.

Saumit spoke for the first time, "There are two real heroes here, Shaitan Singh first and then Ice second. The rest are all almost too good to be true. Having flaws, weaknesses, then overcoming them with fortitude and patience... now that's something! That's what heroes are made of. I salute the flawed and imperfect Shaitan Singh. I also adore Ice for breaking family tradition, exploring new areas, being culturally inept yet secure. I respect him for his ability to identify Shaitan Singh's need and empathize with it. If it wasn't for Ice's risk-taking ability, Shaitan Singh would never have been recognized as a hero." Many applauded Saumit for this outburst.

Indu spoke now, "We will discuss each character at length in a bit but thank you Saumit. Yes, Ice saw beyond Shaitan Singh's Sahayak status and provided him with an opportunity like Dragon and Baaz could see beyond Ice's cultural glitches and trusted him with responsibility. They were all imperfect people as every human being is but it's the nobility of their deeds that justifies their claim on immortality. Don't forget that everyone on that mountain top from both sides of the border did what they believed was right, thereby making each and every one a hero."

"Everyone?" Ishra protested "The enemy were creepy cowards, what they did was wrong and I see no heroism in it...nothing."

Indu's warmth was all-encompassing, "Ishra you must remember that good, bad, right and wrong are subjective terms depending on where you are looking from. It all boils down to perception, Robin Hood may have been a hero to the poor but he was a villain to the rich who he stole from. Similarly, America's attack on Iraq may have been a pre-emptive intervention to protect the world from Weapons of Mass Destruction and bring liberty and freedom to Iraqis but half the world isn't convinced and doesn't agree with that view. One man's militant is another man's freedom fighter."

"True but I don't see how perception can change the truth," Ishra resisted.

"Well Ishra, even truth depends upon perception. Let's take two examples. First one: Most of you kids are health-conscious and starve yourselves to stay in shape. You also study really hard to make a good future for yourself. When your parents find you pushing your limits and studying hard, they praise your willpower but when they see you starving yourself, they are unable to comprehend your mule-headed stubbornness. So are you cursed with stubbornness or are you blessed with willpower? Which is the truth? Or is there a third truth that they are the same?

Second example: A teacher may believe that she is the best because she is passionate and gives her all to her students. She often teaches till late and gets lesser hours at home with her own children. That really pinches her but it's a sacrifice she knowingly makes to be the best. What's more, all her students score the highest marks in every test.

Now ask her students and they may say that their teacher is an incompetent bore because her time management is awful and she loves to hear her own voice and forces them to stay back late everyday while she rants endlessly. They feel that their high grades are not because of her but despite her. They'd do anything to be free of her. Which is the truth? Is she the best or is she an incompetent bore?"

Ishra nodded in agreement, "Yes, I can see where you are going, life is grey, there is no right or wrong and truth depends upon perception."

Indu continued, "So, the enemy soldiers were as passionate

and as dedicated as ours. They did what they needed to do; we were better that night but that doesn't in anyway diminish their commitment or courage."

"Heroes and visionaries are everywhere. Even General Sher Ali Khan would have once been a student just like you. I am certain that this very classroom has an Ice, a Manny and a Shaitan Singh waiting to be triggered. Look within yourself, believe and stand by what you believe in. The world is full of cynics and critics. It's easy to criticize and find fault in everything and everyone around but to seek strength, to stand up for your beliefs, to live by your value system, that's heroism.

It is possible that even your best friend sitting next to you who you spend all day with has probably picked a different favourite from you. For example, Kim picked Ice as her favourite while her childhood friend Sandy picked Sher Ali Khan.

Don't let it surprise you because values are like that, they are personal and you have to choose your own. So let's move forward to my real purpose of telling you this story."

14

ndu continued, "I'd like you to answer the following questions after an open discussion. My questions are:
1. Firstly of course, Ayesha's question. "Why is this story named 'Pride of Lions'?"
2. What have you learnt from this story?
3. What traits of which character have hit you the hardest?
4. What values have you chosen for yourself?
5. How are you going to apply this in your personal life?"

The room came alive with activity as they discussed, argued and debated excitedly among themselves for the next thirty minutes. They would have taken a lot longer if Indu didn't interrupt them and restore order.

When the class finally settled down, Ashiana Mehta was the first to speak. She said, "Ma'am we've brainstormed over all three questions individually and together. We'd now like to present what we have understood and since it's profound, your feedback and guidance is what we really need here."

Indu nodded, "Yes Ashiana, I am here for you."

Ashiana continued, "Since Ayesha asked the first question,

she would now like to answer it herself. Why is this story called the 'Pride of Lions?"

Ayesha spoke, "Ma'am I love the name because it has more than one meaning. The first is that the men in the story are like brave lions who stand up with pride for what they believe in. The second meaning being that the men are like lions and the word to describe a group of Lions is 'pride'. So they are a closely knit pride of Lions who stand by each other against all odds. Also, the soldiers in this incident are mostly Sikhs and all Sikhs end their names with 'Singh' which means Lion!"

"Right you are!" Indu nodded.

Ayesha didn't stop there, she continued, "Ma'am, before you narrated this incident you had said that it's a love story."

"Yes Ayesha I had," Indu said.

"Well Ma'am, I interpreted a love story as a girl-boy romance but you have redefined the term 'love story' for me. This is true and pure love. Thank you Ma'am, I can see that this is probably the best love story I've ever come across. Thank you again Ma'am." Ayesha said and sat down.

Ishra sat comfortably next to Saumit and Nadia. They seemed to have left their little spat behind them. As she spoke now, her excitement was visible, "Ma'am, your second question was 'What have we learnt from this story?' My team and I would like to answer this one. We have learned many things. Some are crystal clear, others are implicit and the rest we have yet to comprehend."

The bell rang unexpectedly, it was like a chainsaw cutting through a heavy oak tree but no one in the class budged. Awestruck, they sat glued to their seats with their full attention on Indu. Her warm and compassionate smile enamoured the class; her eyes seemed to be a universe within which they would gladly lose themselves.

Kiran Bawa spoke up, "1948, 1962, 1965, 1971, Kargil, Tsunamis, riots, terror strikes like 26/11, our army tackles everything, even corruption. I can never forget how Anna Hazare brought the mighty government to its knees in three days flat without raising his voice, firing bullets or blowing anything up. Am so proud to be an Indian and am so proud of our Army."

Kim's hand was up again. Indu looked at her, encouraging her to speak but Sandy and a few others spoke up in chorus drowning out Kim's voice, "Ma'am her father was in the Army." They seemed proud for her. Brij said, "Her father is a decorated army officer; a combat veteran."

Kim said, "Yes but I don't know much because he left before I was born and seldom talks about it. In fact, I got to know about his medals of honour through some of his friends. Then I looked around the home and found boxes with old photographs, many medals, and an exotic collection of daggers."

Sandy said, "Your Dad's a very scary man!"

"Scary?" Kim retorted, "My Dad's a big pushover; he's like a teddy bear."

"Teddy for you, maybe more of a tiger for the rest," Sandy said again and Brij nodded quietly.

Kim said, "Ma'am, you have touched my life irrevocably. I've always practiced most of what you said because my father inculcated values and respect in me since childhood but today you've made me aware that wherever I may be and whatever I may be doing, I still have two very real mothers with me. One is my mother who gave birth to me and the second is my Motherland who I will love, cherish and be proud of forever. Thank you, Ma'am."

Sandy spoke up, "Dad's taking his Mom and my Mom out for dinner tonight and I had dropped out but now I am going to join them and celebrate Mother's day and I'll say a prayer of gratitude in my heart for my Mother India too."

Kim said, "As every year, my Dad's taking me out to dinner to celebrate Mother's Day!"

Brij spoke up, "Ma'am, I really would like to meet Ice and Manny or at least have their email ids if that's possible."

Indu's eyes twinkled like blue diamonds, she flashed a dazzling smile at Brij and said, "Brij, you don't need Ice's email id, I will ensure that you meet him very soon."

Brij was overcome with gratitude. "Thank you Ma'am, thank you for everything. I know my life has changed as of this moment. Is there anything else you would like us to remember or live by?"

"You are all extremely intelligent. I am sure you will forge your own set of rules and your own path but here are five guidelines that you could use till then, they will empower you as human beings." Indu said.

"First: 'Gratitude'. Ambition is good. Aspire for greater heights but stay perpetually grateful for your gifts.

Second: 'Humility'. There will be always someone (no need) richer, better, fancier, younger and more intelligent. Arrogance and ego are the beginning of the end, so stay humble yet excel in every way in everything you do. Genuine humility is a sign of true strength.

Third: 'Respect'. Love and respect yourself, your parents and your country. This love and respect has nothing to do with your bank balance, achievements, branded labels and gadgets. Self-respect and identity are far more profound, spiritual and unshakable. Don't mock or taunt people or things only because you don't understand them. Respect even those who are different, everyone is gifted in their own way. So humility and respect are vital for character building.

Fourth: 'Your inner calling.' We've already discussed living and thinking beyond logic. In Phase 3, the Indians were exhausted and cut off from their supply lines. They were outnumbered, ill-equipped and underfed yet they triumphed over a well-prepared and waiting enemy. Remember, no logic or statistics can stand against the power of the human will."

Fifth: 'Values.' Your values are your moral compass, your code. Create your own set of values and live by them. They determine the fabric of your personality. Navigating the stormy seas of life will be a lot easier once you are clear about your values.

Internalize and live by these five points and you will be rich and wonderful human beings worthy of the abundance that you have. Once you have achieved that stage, the powers that be will bestow many more blessings on you because you will be ready to receive and use these gifts judiciously.

Well my dear children our time is up, I loved every minute of it. Thank you so much. All the best with your project and your journey onward in life, see you soon. Bye, bye."

"Wait!" Sandy said, "Ma'am how do we reach you? When do we see you next?"

Indu said, "Oh don't worry, I am around. We'll keep bumping into each other."

Several students including Ashiana, Ishra, Brij, Kim and Sandy responded with an energetic "Yes, Ma'am!!" and Indu exited the classroom.

Brij spoke first after she was gone. "I've spent my life

believing that logical reasoning holds answers to everything but today I've learnt to go a step beyond. Music and artistry, love, passion and creativity are way beyond rational thinking. Genius begins where logic ends. One cannot lead an ordinary life and expect extra ordinary results. I'm going to train myself to think outside the box, love my mother, my motherland and be grateful for all that I have. I will work towards excelling at everything I do; I will give back to society as much as I can and that's that."

"Am I hallucinating?" A loud voice boomed from the door. All heads turned to see the Principal Mr. Desai standing there.

"Am I to understand that every single one of you has been sitting here unsupervised after Mrs. Maggie left?

Ishra responded, "Sir, We had a substitute teacher, Ms. Indu."

"Nonsense!" Mr. Desai exclaimed. "In fact I almost came here to tell you that your substitute teacher cancelled at the last minute but then I got stuck in a board meeting."

Ashiana Mehta said, "But Sir, Ma'am Indu was here."

Mr. Desai responded, "Indu? Who Indu? We don't have anyone by that name on our faculty or anywhere in this institution!"

All the students stared back in utter surprise at Mr. Desai. He went on, "If this is a scheme to skip your presentations on

Monday, you can forget it! Get packing all of you, no loitering and have a nice weekend."

Flummoxed students slowly picked up their belongings and trickled out of the classroom. Kim, Brij and Sandy were halfway through the hallway when a familiar voice greeted them from behind, "Hi kids!"

The calm tone was unmistakable. It was Kim's favourite person in the whole world. She first shrieked with joy, "Daddy!" Then she turned and ran to hug him. "You remembered our Mother's day dinner!" Kim squealed with joy as her father hugged her back indulgently.

Sandy stiffened instantly; the five-foot seven-inch man who joined them was Veer Nair, Kim's father. He was pleasant and kind but there was something latently dangerous about him. Salt and pepper hair, clean shaven, lean frame, completely fat free, dark complexioned Veer wore a black collared tee shirt tucked into beige cotton slacks with matched beige brogue shoes. He looked like Kim's brother rather than her father. Though he knew Veer since childhood, there was something about him that unnerved Sandy.

"Shall I give you a ride home?"Veer asked.

Kim flashed all her teeth and said, "Yes Daddikins." She hooked one elbow each through Veer and Brij's arms while Veer put an arm around Sandy's shoulder affectionately and the four of them walked out together.

15

As they reached the driveway, Veer's chauffeur-driven limousine swept in. A uniformed aid jumped out and held the passenger door open for them. Brij, Sandy, Kim and Veer made themselves comfortable in the luxurious custom-built vehicle. It allowed plush space for six; three on either side along with a table in between and other essentials like a fridge, printer, fixed telephone lines, etc.

Veer and Kim sat next to each other, Sandy and Brij sat opposite them. Kim narrated to her dad the entire day's happenings and described Indu as the most exquisite and ethereal being she had ever seen. They were interrupted when a fixed phone on the table lit up, Kim knew the caller by the colour of the LED. She reached out and hit the speaker button. "Hi Ajit!" she said. Veer's assistant Ajit Gupte's voice filled the car, "Hi Kim! May I speak with your dad please?"

"Yes Ajit, I'm right here, go ahead," Veer responded from where he sat.

"Sir, Mrs. Preeti Verma, Mr. Rohit Narang and Mr. Ashley Burroughs called to say that they will be attending our celebration party for Ashoka."

Kim interrupted, "Party? What's the party about and what's Ashoka?

Ajit was a kindly sixty-year-old man who had been with Veer since the inception of their company. He adored Kim and treated her like his own daughter. He, like many others, also knew that she would someday take over the reins of Veer's empire.

Ajit replied, "Kim, Ashoka is a firm specializing in intelligence and corporate security. About a decade ago, it was a non-entity till your Dad decided to back it, he in fact pushed Mrs. Verma and Mr. Ashley Burroughs into investing in it. With his support, it grew like a weed and recently crossed the billion dollar mark. That's what the celebration is for and Sir, Mrs. Verma and Mr. Ashley Burroughs specifically asked me to thank you for bullying them into being a part of it."

"Thank you Ajit," Veer said and hit a button disconnecting the call; he then leaned back and gave his complete attention to Kim's chatter. There was nothing Veer enjoyed more than indulging his offspring.

Sandy studied Veer, whose tee shirt sleeve had moved up an inch, and revealed a tattoo. Sandy had seen it before but never from such close quarters. He said, "Nice tattoo sir."

Kim spoke up, sounding like the proud daughter she was, "That's our family's emblem designed by Dad himself and this one on his arm was made by Al, the best tattoo artist there is. Al took sixteen hours to create this masterpiece. This is the first; all the crests you see on our crockery, letterheads and cards are copies of this one." She then pulled up Veer's tee shirt sleeve and revealed the artistry.

Brij and Sandy had seen this motif countless times before. It adorned all of Kim and Veer's cars, offices, and even plaques on their walls. It looked regal but this was the first time they had seen it so close as a tattoo on Veer's arm. Here it appeared to be a lot more than just a crest; it looked visceral, mysterious and seemed to emanate a power of its own.

Brij marvelled at what he saw, the design started from the bottom with a sharp tipped broadsword and rose upward along its blade, halfway through, there seemed to be an ancient medieval plaque with an unintelligible design that looked like a DNA strand in it. Then bursting from either side was a splash of intricate art and an exotic mix of finely interlaced lines forming designs. Sprouting from this splash were two large, gorgeous angel wings rich in texture and filled with detailed brilliantly shaded feathers. He gaped at the exquisite mastery and his eyes scrolled further up as the angel wings unfurled vertically and ended in what looked like Phoenix wing tips at Veer's shoulder. Back to the centre of the blade, further up beyond the plaque and the wings was an exotic Gothic or Viking-like handle.

"What's that?" Sandy hesitatingly asked, his attention was at the centre of the artwork that sprouted halfway through the sword's blade. He took Brij's phone, switched on a 'torch app' and shone its bright light directly on the tattoo. He then leaned closer and ran his finger along the area outlining another pattern within the larger one.

"You are really sharp Sandy!" Veer complimented.

Brij too leaned forward; Sandy was right... there was a much shorter dagger-like blade hidden inside the long broad sword and within the large angel wings, he saw a set of much smaller wings again well- concealed by overlaying the larger artwork. That wasn't all, Brij and Sandy noticed that the overlaying lines also cleverly cloaked what appeared to be a horizontal scar running across Veer's arm.

There were faded stitch marks along the old scar, easy to miss but on close inspection, they looked like those you'd find on a gurney sack of rice or wheat more than on a human being. Sandy deduced that these stitches must have been hurriedly and crudely done probably on some battlefield with no painkillers. It must have been painful but the scar looked august now.

Brij's brain was in hyper drive, he snatched his phone from Sandy, turned off the torch and began surfing to seek answers. He had seen the inner insignia somewhere before and searched the innermost recesses of his mind and the internet for it.

Veer pulled his sleeve back down and there was silence as they drove on. It was almost ten whole minutes before Brij's expression changed and he exclaimed loudly, "Kavvach!" meaning 'Armour'.

"What?" Sandy asked.

Ignoring Sandy, Brij continued, "Oh my God... Sir, you were part of a 'Kavvach' unit! I've only heard of such people as phantoms and read books about them. I have never come even close to a real person from a 'Kavvach' unit."

Sandy and Kim looked questioningly at Brij who excitedly continued, "Kim, the family crest is fantastic but it hides something more! Concealed within is the logo of the elite Kavvach unit. Your dad is one in a million!"

"Of course he is!" Kim said defensively.

Brij ploughed on, "No. No. I mean literally! Every year about five hundred thousand people apply for the Army officer entrance exam. Not more than a hundred thousand make it though the written level. Those who do are sent for a twelve-day psychological evaluation. Of that hundred thousand, not even one thousand are cleared. Those who do, go for a physical exam. More than seventy percent flunk there!

The remaining three hundred are sent for medical checkups and it's hardly a hundred which clear that level.

These lucky hundred guys go for officer training which lasts anything from ten months to a year and a half during which at least another twenty drop out or fail. So hardly eighty become army officers out of the original five hundred thousand who apply!

"Wow!" Kim gasped.

"Wait that's not all," Brij continued, "Not more than one or two out of each batch of seventy five get into Specfore unit and they too have a rigorous probation period with a fifty percent failure rate!"

"Really?" Kim exclaimed.

Brij went on, breathless with excitement. "Kavvach men were handpicked from the Specfore. That means Kim, your dad is literally one in a million!"

Kim choked with pride and looked at her dad who seemed amused and impressed.

Sandy thought long and hard and after several minutes, he turned to Kim and Brij with an expression of shock and disbelief. Kim asked, "What is it Sandy?"

Sandy waited till Veer looked at him and then in a tentative tone, he asked "Sir, did you have a nickname in the army?" "Yes Son, I did." Veer answered.

Almost in a trance-like state, Sandy asked again but this time his voice cracked as he spoke. He had to clear his throat and ask, "Sir, was your army nickname 'Ice'?"

Veer seemed pleasantly surprised.

"Why yes, it was! How on earth did you know that?"

Kim intervened, "Wait a minute. Dad, you are Ice? How is that possible?"

"Yep that was my nickname," Veer said with a smile. "How did you know that, Sandy?"

Sandy's excitement had peaked, he was bursting with glee. "Indu said that Ice was in a Kavvach unit and that the .50 calibre ripped through his Kavvach tattoo! Don't you see? The scar on your Dad's arm is exactly where Ice got hit by the heavy machine gun fire on Ring Contour! Think about it, how many Kavvach operatives can there be of the same age from Mumbai with the scar on the exact same place? He has to be Ice! And Indu said we would meet Ice soon!!"

"Impossible!" Brij exclaimed in disbelief.

"Why impossible?" Sandy asked.

"But you are not a Sikh! You are not even a North Indian!" Brij shot back in disbelief at Veer.

Veer said, "Brij, we were a team. There was no North, East, West or South; there was no religion, caste, creed or colour, we were Indians. We were bonded seamlessly together as one unit, no leaders or followers; we trusted each other, played our roles did the best we could."

Kim said "Dad..."

"Yes Kim?"

"This company called Ashoka that you believed in so much that you bullied your friends to invest in it. Does it belong to Sergeant Major Manvinder Singh, Manny?"

"Yes it does Kim." Veer replied.

Brij leaned back and laughed out loud, more out of disbelief than amusement and then he turned to Kim and asked, "Kim, how did you figure this one out? How did you get to Manny being the owner of Ashoka?"

Kim said, "Manny is a Sikh, all Sikh names end with Singh and Singh means Lion. The pillar of Ashoka is the Indian National symbol it has four lions…pride of lions, right Dad?" She asked Veer.

"Elementary, my dear Watson!" Veer chuckled.

Sandy sat dumbfounded, taking it all in. He watched Kim and Veer who sat opposite him. They both wore their watches on the right hand, some kind of absurd family tradition, both had a penchant for earthy colours in their clothing; they were like two peas in a pod.

They rode in silence for a while before Kim's facial colour changed again as realization dawned on her. She had made a huge revelation. "Ohhhh!" She said out aloud, "We are so stupid! All of us! She was right with us and we didn't know it!"

"Who?" Sandy asked, "What are you blabbing about?"

Kim replied, "Our mother, everyone's mother!"

Sandy was exasperated, "Mother? Whose mother? God Kim you aren't making any sense....explain quickly!"

"Indu!" Kim yelled, "Indu! Can't you see who she really was?"

"No. I can't," Sandy said. "No." Brij said in chorus.

"Let me break it down for you." Kim said as Sandy and Brij listened impatiently. "Mr. Desai said there was no substitute teacher today. He said there was no Indu anywhere on the rolls. Right? "He was right...," Kim said, "Think about it....what did Indu wear?"

"A sari," Brij said and Sandy added, "...a simple white and orange sari with a green blouse, very pretty. No embroidery, very chic."

Kim jumped in, "Not orange, saffron. It was white with a saffron border and a green blouse. The colours of our national flag. Her blue eyes were the *chakra* of our flag."

"Her name Indu stands for India, - the Indus Valley Civilization. She said the story was about her children, we are all her children. No wonder she knew all our names!"

"Yeah she did know all our names!" Brij exclaimed loudly.

"Indu was a manifestation of our mother India, she is an

idea transformed into life. Most people of our generation have no concept of love for the country or values. Values aren't even a subject in school or college! She must have been hurt by our loss of direction and self-respect, don't you see? So she manifested as Indu and visited us on Mother's Day to set us back on course, she was here to guide us."

Sandy stared back. His face showcased incredulity. He finally replied, "That's ridiculous!"

"Is it? Prove me wrong," Kim said.

Sandy fell silent, he couldn't argue with Kim, her theory was farfetched but was watertight; Kim looked at her father who was lost in thought looking at the traffic outside. She asked him "What do you think Dad?" Veer looked back at her expressionlessly and she realized that he hadn't heard a thing. His hearing was slightly impaired; it came and went as it pleased. Sometimes he could hear well and sometimes he missed every word spoken.

During her growing up years, Kim's responses to Veer's hearing impairment varied from displays of extreme exasperation to unabashed love and adulation but now she knew how it happened and was overwhelmed.

Brij thought hard and remembered Indu's advice of going beyond logic. No wonder Kim figured things out faster than the rest. Even now, her theory made sense, Indu really did know everyone's names, in fact, she seemed to know almost everything about everyone. He finally spoke. "I may have to agree with Kim, it's a known fact that when enough people believe genuinely with all their heart and soul in something... anything, then that idea can become reality."

Kim glanced at her father who sat next to her, still lost in his own world. She was about to look away when something struck her and she looked at him again. 'Wait a minute, is he smiling?' Kim, Sandy and Brij looked at each other, then back at Veer. Maybe he did hear everything they said. 'Is that a reflection of light or are his eyeballs looking as blue as Indu's right now?'

"Oh, My God!" All three gasped out loud, "His eyes are blue!"